The
Carapace Caper

In Africa with Anstruther Carapace

WENDY VEEVERS-CARTER

iUniverse, Inc.
New York   Bloomington

The Carapace Caper
In Africa with Anstruther Carapace

iUniverse books may be ordered through booksellers or by contacting:

iUniverse
1663 Liberty Drive
Bloomington, IN 47403
www.iuniverse.com
1-800-Authors (1-800-288-4677)

ISBN: 978-1-4502-3872-4 (pbk)
ISBN: 978-1-4502-3873-1 (cloth)
ISBN: 978-1-4502-3874-8 (ebk)

Printed in the United States of America

iUniverse rev. date: 9/16/2010

to the grandchildren

LIST OF ILLUSTRATIONS

-

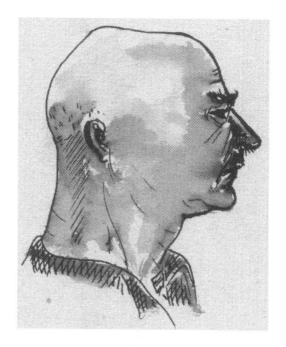

Anstruther Carapace

In 1953, Prudence and I, twenty-one and fresh out of college, arrived in Nairobi to take up a job with the explorer-scientist Anstruther Carapace. The job was to assist him on two films he was making. One was to be called "The Jungle Night," and the other "The Undersea World." We were to share the small salary offered. The big draw was the trip to Africa.

It was early morning when we got to Nairobi. The highlands of Kenya have a pleasant climate, but I was hot. My mother had insisted on sending me off "properly dressed" (for New York) and carrying a winter coat, and because in those days the baggage allowance was very restricted, the pockets of the coat were full of small but heavy items while others had been sewn into the lining to avoid paying excess charges. Mother stopped short of adding a solar topee (with net) at my insistence that such things must be readily available in Nairobi. I was privately determined not to wear one.

Prudence was much less laden. Her family were no more sensible than mine, but they were less determined. Faced with literally endless possibilities, they ended up doing nothing. Lucky Pru.

The idea of going to Africa started with the rubber stamp Anstruther had left behind in his room— he often stayed with us when he was in New York. Printed, it announced:

The Tropical Tree Tops
The Jungle Night
The Undersea World

I gazed at these invitations to adventure. Ansti (as we called him) had been in the Congo only last year with some sort of tree-climbing contraption, and he was always going off to somewhere like the Congo or New Guinea to film some unusually large crocodile or rare marsupial; using our house as a staging post. Ropes and harnesses, even a diving helmet would appear just inside our front door on his, and their, way somewhere. I envied him.

Then, in my senior year at Radcliffe, studying anthropology, I got this letter:

Dec.4 1952.
Dear Wendy

I am making plans to return to East Africa in June for about a year's work with the jungle spot light for about 6 months and then below the Red Sea.

Perhaps you know a Radcliffe girl I could get for this expedition. She should swim + dive, and photograph well. The undersea part is the more important, and should be much like the part of Lotte Berl in the current R.K.O. picture — Below the Red Sea.

I signed myself up at once. I wasn't all that photogenic. Presentable maybe, but no beauty. On the other hand, I reasoned, Ansti couldn't have expected to find Hollywood starlets at Radcliffe. What a chance! Africa! A ticket to Africa! My mother said she would have preferred graduate school or at least what she called a "*proper* expedition." She said she wouldn't stand in my way, but she absolutely would not allow me to go alone. Anstruther Carapace, inventor, tinkerer, explorer and, amateur film maker, might be a familiar figure to me (as a child) but my mother had known him from *her* childhood. Back in Cambridge I got another note:

Dear Wendy,

Glad to hear about the two Radcliffe girls. I believe such a party should get more interresting publicity. [I retain Anstruther's spelling.] …I am a little worried about finances and pay for two. I must purchase a Power Wagon to replace or supplement my station wagon [left in the Congo]…A round trip ticket to Nairobi or Costermansville by air is about $1500.

Possibly we could go together to Egypt on a cabin freighter and then up the Nile with the truck…

I would have agreed to anything. And I had a like-minded friend (Louise, then, not Pru). I tried to explain Anstruther to Louise. It was no use expecting him to behave normally, I told her. A normal scientist photographing animals at night for one film and then fish and underwater scenes in the Red Sea for another would not be employing two 21 year old tyros in the first place. This was a chance to see Africa.

If Anstruther was eccentric—all right, a little crazy—so what? Louise was very relaxed about this and as keen on adventure as I was.

In February, Ansti wrote saying he thought it would take two months to get the power wagon to Mombasa or maybe Dar-es-Salaam and would book "Barbara" (Louise) and me to arrive with the truck. The next letter suggested I "learn lariat," adding we will not ask you to lassoe [sic] lions, elephants or leopards. Buffaloes, rhinos, larger antelopes, yes." On the back was a drawing of the power wagon, two people on the top, a spotlight, a net with the tag "smaller animals get net," and a very small rhino about to run into the noose of a lasso. A note near the rhino added that a kedge anchor, lashed to a fender, would be secured to the lariat's bitter end as "break [sic] on escaping animal."

March 16 [1953] (Another letter from Ansti)
    I talked to Pete and Mary (his brother-in-law and sister) about Africa. They agree with me that you may like it and be very good as an explorer. On the other hand they think that due to pink and white complexion or other alergy [!] you may be ill or not be happy about so much camp life…About a month ago explorer Giles Healey brought me pictures of Gwen Randall of Los Angeles, Scotch, square-jawed, 27, experienced as bit player, and champ swimmer. I have never seen her, but she did write me a letter saying how much she would like to go to Africa even though she has to leave her son behind…
    I cannot afford to pay for more than one girl, and wish definitely to make you first choice. But if you should care to take her [Gwen R.] instead of Louise it may have some advantages, and believe you and she would make a good team. However she might not be keen on working on with me if you got sick…

With hindsight, this might indeed have been a good idea. Ah, hindsight!

In May, Louise suddenly changed her mind about Africa and decided she was going to get on a freighter, go to Japan and marry her boyfriend stationed there. So I asked Prudence. I never gave a thought to the mature twenty-seven year old stranger Ansti had mentioned. Prudence was a schoolmate and seemed the right sort. As with Louise, the arrangement was that we would share the salary Ansti offered ($5 a day. I knew he wouldn't get a Hollywood starlet for that). We were unconcerned with the details.

By the end of May, however, although I was concentrating on my final exams, I did try to get more information out of Ansti. I made out a questionnaire leaving spaces for his answers.

1. Mother says you are going to be in Boston for a week sometime. When is this? (I wanted to talk to him.)

"I shall be here today and some more perhaps." (Not what I wanted to know: "here" was New York.)

2. Can I see movie you have made sometime? When? Where? (This was an unfinished diving film Ansti had been working on sporadically for years. To complete it was the purpose of the Red Sea part of the expedition.)

"Perhaps K [my mother] can come. We can get it projected here [New York] or for less in Boston." (I never did see it.)

3. Can I see the Power Wagon before it is shipped off?

"If you go to Pier 3, Erie Basin, Brooklyn…I can take you." (I was in Cambridge.)

4. What equipment should be gotten here and what in Nairobi or Costermansville? (Ansti hadn't yet decided whether to fly to Kenya or the Congo.)

"I am trying to avoid paying air freight. You are allowed 65 lbs." Mosquito netting?
"I'll look into this. They are light."
Bedroll?
"Nairobi."
Clothing?
"Nairobi or here. 65 lbs. Get two buckle army boots at A & N. There is one in Central Square, Cambridge.

5. I plan on getting so far: two buckle boots, white bathing suit [the original girl had worn a white one piece bathing suit. Ansti said this would provide "continuity"]

"I'll give you 2 bottles of chloroquin."

6. Anything else? What about a pistol in addition to rifles? [We were reading about the Mau Mau insurgency in the papers]

"O.K. but 65 lbs. Can get it in Nairobi if needed for protection."

7. I am going to learn to shoot /lasso in Boston this month.

"Good…Why don't you take out a gun license in Nairobi? I have shotgun and .22 rifles. If you want high power rifle I'll air freight or get it to Nairobi if you take out license there."

8. Should we have shoes for walking on bottom of Red Sea with helmet on, and what kind if so; and should we have flippers as in "Under the Red Sea" for free swimming with the mask?

"I have flippers. We'll get chieper [sic] shoes for this

9.. What do you think of the idea of getting some foam rubber, cutting it to fit, and using it to protect bare shoulders when using the helmet? We need something of the sort. (The helmet was the heavy old-fashioned type normally attached to a diving suit.)

"Let's get regular shoulder pads at Morse Diving on Atlantic Ave. I plan to assemble all diving gear next week…wonder how I can collect helmet. No car."

10… What sort of arrangement is to be made about the payment of the salary?

"Your salary starts the day you leave. I would be glad if you wish to go calling in Nairobi to have you do so, but salary should be skipped. You may do good calling around…" Anstruther was to change his mind about this.

The next letter, in June, came from Kampala.

"I hope this finds you and Patricia [Prudence] well and enthusiastic. I just got here today with all luggage except one chest left at border with Hindoo express company…plan to clear truck in Mombasa late this week…Here's a bit of Egyptian money for you. Looking forward to seeing you June 30."

Prudence and I flew first to England (12 hours in a prop plane with a refuelling stop at Gander: there were no jets then), and the next day on via Malta (an overnight stop) to Khartoum where we changed planes at 2 A.M. for Nairobi. I remember how dry Africa looked from the air, and not just over the Sudan. By seven, we had come down out of the clouds and were flying near the edge of a vast plateau; we guessed that the steep drop to the right must be the Rift Valley escarpment. A few hills and updrafts later, we landed at Nairobi where everything seemed to be either covered with or made of red soil, including the surprisingly smooth runway. We were at once confronted by a lot of fussy British rules and regulations to comply with, and a rigid hierarchy of personnel to enforce them: Immigration, British, Customs, Indian; the Africans were porters or guards.

Ansti turned up, very dusty, having driven up from Mombasa. He was in a good humor and was quite witty at the expense of the immigration officer who had ascertained by various means that he was in the colony illegally. Luckily Immigration was a nice young man with a lenient spirit. He let us all into Kenya when we were able to prove "financial stability:" No poor whites were allowed into the colony.

Ansti said he had a lot of people to report to—red tape, he said dismissively—but took us first to a tall gloomy hotel, very Victorian, on what appeared to be Nairobi's main street, Delamere Avenue. He said we'd have to move out of town the next day: "no place to pack the gear here." No place to park either: we circled Lord Delamere's statue three times before finding a space. He planned to leave Nairobi in a day or two, if he didn't get too "taped up."

So—we had a chance to look around. As a first step, we looked up Prudence's father's Standard Oil introduction. This proved to be a good idea as this man immediately assigned a Mrs. Travers to show us around and tell us where to get things. She told us about Lord Delamere and took us to the bank, the post office and the bookstore. Every office or shop was staffed by Indians, and on the streets the Indian women in their colourful saris were a contrast to the peculiarly dowdy brand of Englishwoman that had come out here. The streets looked very peaceful and quiet, here in the center of town anyway, but we noticed that even so nearly every Britisher, male or female, was armed with a gun or a knife, the gun in a holster on a belt, the knife stuck in the top of the knee-length stockings the men wore with their shorts. In contrast, the Africans looked very relaxed and happy; they laughed a lot and had the most enchanting smiles. The streets were clean, much cleaner than in New York. It was pleasantly cool at about 5000 feet above sea level. We saw very few beggars or peddlers. The general impression was modern, dusty, a bit dull. We passed one square entirely filled with Africans squatting on their heels, waiting for something. There were very few other Americans, or tourists of any kind. Mrs. Travers asked what we needed and when we mentioned getting things for safari, she took us to Ahmed & Co., a huge place full of khaki clothes, tents and rolls of cloth and canvas for making more. She said, "They'll make anything."

The next morning the hotel was buzzing. In the night, a white man, just up from Mombasa and looking into a shop window, had been shot by a native policeman, who then ran up an alley and shot himself. All the British in the hotel were talking about it. No motive had been discovered, but no one seemed much alarmed. They all said that the native must have gone berserk. They scoffed at the idea of real danger in Nairobi, explaining that the bad areas were around Mt. Kenya. They assured us that Tanganyika (as it was then), where Ansti said we were going, was perfectly safe. The general opinion was that the whole thing (the Mau Mau rebellion) had been talked up rather much. Nothing like this shooting had ever happened in daytime in the city. On the other hand, we learned that most "nice" people lived well outside the city on isolated farms, and many had settled in the rift valley and the so-called "white highlands" where Mau Mau attacks were increasing.

Ansti did not reappear until the dessert course of lunch, looking very grey but from engine grease rather than illness. He ate all seven courses—seven! From number one, something called "first toasties," through soup, a bit of dried up fish, some grey meat, overcooked vegetable, dessert , to "second toasties," each "course" served separately, and very slowly by waiters in long white robes with red sashes around their waists and red fezzes on their heads—while he talked to us about "Jungle Nighting" and the state of the Weak Sister. The Weak Sister was the Willys jeep station wagon he had had just collected from the Congo. The waiters stared at our table fixedly. We were the last in the dining room, a pattern Anstruther invariably managed to repeat in towns, though he was keen enough on prompt meals on safari, he told us.

"You girls gotta keep the chuck wagon going on safari," he

instructed, "and none of this fancy stuff, hotels and so on, Spoil you," he added, looking from our clean clothes to his grimy shorts. We didn't pay much attention. The words "on safari" had triggered their own pictures in our minds which had nothing to do with chuck wagons.

The next day we moved out of town to a sort of motel on the outskirts of Nairobi. It was a pretty place. The bougainvillea was aflame everywhere, thorny branches even stretching over the tall power wagon that we were soon disembowelling onto the motel's clean drive. "Working clothes today," Ansti had warned us early in the morning, and we saw why. The power wagon was thick in red dust from the Mombasa road, and we were too as soon as we started to undo the canvas cover. Ansti had designed the back of the power wagon to consist of a rigid expanded metal cage welded to the 18 inch sides. The cage was covered by a canvas tarpaulin similar to a land rover's with lots of thimbles for lashing it down. At the rear were two expanded metal doors with their own drop-down canvas cover. Thimbles on this and the main cover provided for lashing the two together. We could see that once loaded and sewn up, the back of the wagon was not something to be opened for any little thing one might have forgotten. Leftovers as well as ready-access things like rope, spare tires, jacks and the battered chuck box would travel in the Weak Sister.

These two vehicles, a big spotlight, a small spotlight, a mattress (for the cameraman and the light holder to sit on while filming, not for sleeping on), three camp beds and a small satchel each was what Ansti planned on carrying, apart from drums of fuel and oil and spares. The big generator for the light occupied most of the power wagon's carrying capacity. When asked, Ansti said bedding, even a tent, was unnecessary—mere soft living. All right, he agreed, other safaris had tents. So what?

But if it rains?

"Listen," he said, "this is Africa. You know when it is going to rain. You got camp beds, haven't you? Keep you off the ground. Pull 'em under the jeep or the power wagon, or get in the jeep and sleep there. What's the worry?"

We looked at all the square edged things already inside the jeep and sighed, but we were even less anxious to interfere with Ansti's claim on the interior of the greasy power wagon as his own bed chamber. As a trial, we tried setting up one of the camp beds and getting it under the

Willys. Its bent iron legs didn't push easily, and when we got it under there was only just clearance for the bed without a body on it. Still, we were assured by some of our fellow guests at the motel that the rains didn't begin until November. Indeed, those were just the "short rains;" the long rains were from February to April or May. In July we were obviously going to be dry enough.

"You want to worry more about carrying enough water with you than about getting wet," a farmer told us. "Lots of people go out with only a couple of jerry cans and then can't find water when they're stuck. Water, that's the worry in Africa," he said, watching the dust clouds that followed every car along the road.

We broached the subject of water with Ansti, but he returned the ball. He had a barrel. It was an evil, diesel-smelling barrel whose top never fitted properly, we found out later. But—he had a barrel. Not finding anything more to test him with, we finished the loading and went for a wash. Ansti said we'd be leaving for Tanganyika Territory soon. Time to get a duffel bag made at Ahmed & Co., buy a Swahili dictionary, write letters, go to the museum, talk to the other people at the hotel. One man guffawed loudly when we described the idea of the Jungle Night, and told us about Carr Hartley's animal farm "where all you people go." We were edgy about being lumped in the category of rich American film people (we need not have worried) but encouraged him to tell us more. I'd never met anyone who actually guffawed.

Jungle Night Tonight, Girls

On the 4th of July, we loaded up early and left Nairobi, Ansti drove the power wagon. Pru and I followed in the Weak Sister. We took the Mombasa road until the Athi River, or rather a signboard in the middle of the dry flat red plains that said it was the Athi River, then branched off for Arusha. We saw our first ostriches. The African space was impressive: miles and miles of open dry grassland dotted with thorn trees, hills in the distance, and plenty of animals —giraffes, zebras, antelopes, wildebeest — grazing under an immense blue sky. We wanted to stop to photograph all this, but the power wagon roared on and we didn't dare get left behind.

Wildebeest on the Kapiti plains

By early afternoon, we were wilting from the steady hot driving and the swallowing of Ansti's dust, so we were pleasantly surprised to see him turn off the road onto a curved drive signed "The Namanga Hotel," and stop in front of a thatched bungalow surrounded by trees. Possibly we were going to have *tea*? Ansti, we had already noticed, was fond of his tea. Had the slightly English traditions of his native Boston encouraged this taste? (The Carapaces were an old Boston family.) In any case, the institution was inescapable in East Africa. It might consist of badly made (boiled) black tea, dry bread sandwiches or a piece of tinned cake, but everyone stopped to have tea.

Just as we were developing this theory, Ansti emerged from the shadows inside the entrance. "We got to stay here tonight, it seems," he announced dolefully. "The park [the nearby Amboseli Game Reserve] isn't open after four and I want to see that warden. Want to film there tonight. Guess you girls can unpack now. But lock up tight when you've finished and we'll go for a walk."

Our first walk in Africa. You couldn't count Nairobi. This was the African bush. Our parents' cautionary words came back to us. We had our boots on, of course, laced up high against snake bite, our levis tucked well into them, long-sleeved shirts, bandannas for our hair, sunglasses on and plenty of insect repellent. A pity, we thought, that the repellent had no effect on the flies. Prudence put the snake bite kit in her pocket. Ansti set off down a road deep in red dust with us following, but soon turned off. Thorn tree scrub, a rock pile or two, nothing of a view; it was certainly snaky looking country. We kept our eyes busily on the ground.

"I wonder if all those big rhinos know they're supposed to stay in the game park." Ansti said musingly, looking at us, which gave us something more than snake bite to worry about. Rhinos, we'd been told in Nairobi, charge anything. "Look like a tank coming down on you. Course, there's a trick'd be useful to you if you're going out in the bush. Y'can't outrun 'em, y'see. Just remember t'stand still and when they come down on you jump to the left."

"Whose left?" I had asked.

"Oh — er…well, you're facing 'em, so must be your left — no, I remember, it's the rhino's left so it must be your right because the rhino, see, always leads with the right foot and can't turn to his left so quick-like."

We digested this.

"Or is it that he can't see so well on one side?" our informant reflected. "Well, anyway, remember to jump," he said cheerfully as he left us.

"I think rhinos must make a lot of noise coming," said Pru slowly. "Hardly anything attacks them so they don't creep about much, I think."

Before the reserve's gates shut, we drove in to see the warden. Immediately inside the entrance we saw our very first rhino posing in front of a distant snow-topped Kilimanjaro, but Ansti wouldn't stop. He made straight for Ol Tukai, the warden's camp. Here he had a long argument with the warden that we kept out of. Eventually the warden must have given in because he told one of the game scouts to go back with us to the entrance to tell the guard there we had permission to come back in after dark. Ansti assured the warden that he knew his way around the reserve having been there before.

Back at the hotel, we got the mattress lashed onto the roof of the power wagon while Ansti tested the generator, the spotlight and the camera. We had something to eat then drove back to the reserve. We hadn't been inside ten minutes before Ansti announced that we were lost. "But don't worry about it. We'll take a bearing on Kilimanjaro, find the warden's camp and get the road from there." His voice trailed off. He was concentrating on the difficulty of getting wild animals to fit into his plans. A big herd of zebras had come into sight. "Up to the roof, Wendy." (I was assigned the light that day, Prudence the driving). Ansti clambered into the back and started the generator.. The light came on and the zebras actually did freeze, dazzled. "Hold the beam on them!" Ansti clambered over the roof with his camera to join me on the mattress. He hammered on the cab roof. "Drive closer!" he yelled to Prudence. We approached, lumberingly. The noise of the generator was deafening. The zebras "broke dazzle" and rushed away. "Follow, follow!" Ansti yelled. "What?" asked Pru sticking her head out of the window. "Follow the zebra! Hurry!" This provided an exciting ride, but no photos. We spent the next hours cruising around, looking for other game to dazzle until we were all tired and discouraged. Fortunately we came upon the main park track by accident.

Next day, we drove on to Arusha and booked into a dusty-looking place called the Safari House Hotel; even Ansti didn't camp in towns. We gratefully washed off the dust and sweat and went downstairs for a cold beer. Tusker beer came in very unladylike-sized bottles but we were developing quite a taste for it. A day swallowing red dust turned it into nectar. We were soon joined by some other people staying there, all men, who introduced themselves and wanted to know what we were doing in Arusha. One man said he was a white hunter, our first, outside of those we'd read about in Hemingway, and we looked at him critically. There were two young "commercial" types who worked in Arusha, and a man who said he was the local game ranger. After at least two rounds of beer, Ansti appeared, scowling at the sight of all the bottles and (maybe) the men. We suggested he join us. He said he didn't drink beer. "I'm ready to eat," he announced. We told him, rather airily, that we would eat later,

Looking back, it may be that our relations with Ansti started to deteriorate from this moment, but were we really obliged to eat with him? Besides, we were getting all sorts of valuable information and advice from these experienced safari types, all of them incredulous at Ansti's apparent lack of plans and his rudimentary camping gear. Undoubtedly they put ideas in our heads. No tents? No *boys*? You girls *do the cooking*? They were speechless. *No one* did without boys in Africa. When they found we didn't even have bedrolls, they were stupefied. We were obviously ignorant, so the "old man" (Ansti) got all the blame, and we had offers of help from them all. We found this very pleasant.

They must have discussed the queer Carapace safari over more beer after we'd gone upstairs. Tony, one of the commercials (with Shell Oil), said he'd take care of getting the bedrolls made. The white hunter had to leave early in the morning, but the game ranger gallantly agreed to look after us, take us to his area, show us around. *He* had tents and boys, of course. No problem there. The next morning, this plan was presented to Ansti as an admirable program, even as the means of making a successful film. It sounded very good for the expedition, as we told him. Free boys, equipment, and a guide to good places for Jungle Nighting. Could he object?

He couldn't really. But he was grumpy and accepted the help very grudgingly I told Pru this was "just Ansti." It wasn't as if he had any plan of his own beyond a vague one of going to the Serengeti, the huge new national park northwest of Arusha.

The game ranger, Oliver Fenton, was, we judged, about forty, darkly tanned, with an amused, tolerant expression on his face and as we soon found out a lot of experience in places other than Africa under his belt. We bought food for the safari, tinned stuff mostly, and some beer. We wrote hasty letters home and the next day set off behind Oliver's beat-up old land rover, heading towards his base at Mtu-wa-Mbu ("River of Mosquitoes") where he would put us up for the night. The Weak Sister was left behind in Arusha. After a few hours on the road, we stopped at a *duka* (shop) to buy a couple of live chickens for supper.

Oliver's place was an airy bungalow a couple of miles off the road which led to the famous Ngorongoro crater, and on the eponymous river, a fine river falling over rocks and swirling through deep pools. We all (except Ansti, busy with something in

Oliver (with a sore toe)

the depths of the power wagon) went for a swim as soon as we got there. Big trees, cool water: bliss. Things were looking up. Eventually Oliver's cook produced food, a different sort of Bad British to the version in hotels, but we weren't complaining. We drank beer cooled in the river and listened to Oliver's stories about life in Burma and China, where he'd been in the war. He planned to take us south to a place called Nondotto, good open country for Jungle Nighting, he assured us, with lots of game. Ansti didn't say much, but remarked on a fine tree he'd seen on the way up to the house "just right for a gorilla to throw a girl out of." Oliver raised his mobile eyebrows and winked at us. Throwing girls out of trees indeed. Fortunately all Ansti had so far made us do, besides drive the vehicles and handle the spotlight, was to "practice lariat" by perching us in trees at the motel in Nairobi while he ran, shoulders hunched, underneath. To his disappointment we were not good at all good at this.

Masai women

Nondotto proved to be a Masai encampment and the flies were horrific. Night time was the only respite. The Masai were so used to them they didn't even brush them away but let them crawl all over their skins and cluster in the corners of their eyes, and of their babies' eyes which festered with the irritation. It was hard to get used to this although the compensation was learning a lot about the Masai way of life. The women and children were very friendly and sat close beside us whenever they and we had nothing else to do. Every evening, the men and boys returned with the cattle in clouds of dust, herding them into the thorn brush enclosure surrounding the hide-covered huts. The high wall of thorn brush, Oliver explained, kept both people and animals safe from lions, evidently something of a pest in this area. Oliver was on very good, even familiar, terms with these Masai and daily received a large gourd of fresh milk from one or another of the bead-covered nubile girls. The gourd, he explained, was always rinsed with cow urine to keep it fresh. Ansti, who had already told us in America that he never camped near native villages—"hotbeds of contagion" he called them—naturally did not care for any of this, but had to concede (we supposed) that Oliver was good about the after-dark Jungle Night outings, taking us to different places every night. We encountered a lot of small animals to dazzle though no lion. Ansti didn't complain, except about the bully beef which appeared every night for supper.

"The secret of success in the army is a liking for bully beef," he announced loudly on the third day, pushing the stuff around his tin plate. Oliver's boys didn't do anything with the stringy beef, just added it to roughly mashed potatoes and boiled cabbage.. I don't know why Oliver didn't shoot something edible like an antelope. Perhaps he couldn't be bothered. He spent a lot of time talking to Prudence, and I could see that she liked him.

The jungle night outings gradually became better organised, and Ansti must have got quite good footage of dazzled hyenas, wild dogs, and even a leopard, once. But though we could hear lion grunting, but we never saw any, and there were no rhino or buffalo or elephants, or if there were, they were warned off by the noise we made. Without big game it was difficult to imagine that shots of startled wildlife could make a successful film, but that was Ansti's problem, not ours. We spent two or three hours every night rumbling around in the power wagon, the generator hammering away, with Oliver in the cab directing the route. One night, when Pru was on top, she forgot to hold onto the net well enough and it fell off somewhere, but Oliver's boys found it the next day. After about a week, on one of the nights when Prudence was driving and there was a lull in activity, she told me Oliver proposed to her. Later, in our tent, she said she was *seriously considering* this idea. Wow! Quick work, Oliver! He was indeed charming with a nice sense of humour, but wasn't he a little old? We didn't tell Ansti. There was a lot of safari time still ahead of us.

The day after The Proposal, Oliver said we had to go to Kibaya to get water. He explained that the only water hole with pure water in this area was near Kibaya, but there was no track, just a cow path, to get there. Oliver said that if Ansti would take the power wagon to collect two barrels full (which the land rover could not carry), we could see how many branches the boys needed to cut along this cow path to allow the power wagon with the big light mounted on top to get through for a "night run." Kibaya was on the way back to Arusha and Ansti planned to return there, jungle-nighting at the same time, to pick up the Willys jeep before going to the Serengeti.

Kibaya was only about 16 miles from Nondotto but it took us all day to complete the round trip and we returned to camp shaken and bruised. Ansti went at top speed through the dense thorn bush, and each time the boys piled out to chop branches with their big pangas, he would wait impatiently, one foot on the accelerator, and as soon as the path was clear, start off with a roar. The boys in front would scatter frantically and join those behind running to catch up. Prudence, Oliver and I had chosen to make the trip standing on the tailgate flap, much cooler than the hot cab. We held onto the top of the cage whose doors had been removed, and with our free hands pulled the boys on board as they reached us. This scene was repeated many times.

On the way back, the boys no longer had to clear the path so they wedged themselves into the back and tried to hold the drums of fuel and the two drums of water each weighing about 450 pounds steady between their feet. The first time Ansti stopped for something, we jumped off to tell him he just had to go more slowly, but we had only reached the door of the cab when he roared off again, disappearing down the cow path in a cloud of dust. Oliver reckoned we were 13 miles from camp and that Ansti would never know we weren't on board. Oliver's boys told him later they'd shouted themselves hoarse from inside the truck, and some of them jumped off too. Fortunately for us, a side mirror and a windshield wiper were ripped off a mile or two further on and Ansti discovered we were missing.

In another couple of days, Ansti decided we'd exhausted the possibilities of the Nondotto area and that in spite of the clearing of the Kibaya track the surrounding bush was much too thick for photography to think of returning to Arusha that way. Oliver said he had to go on somewhere else, so we broke camp and went back to Arusha by road, camping one night near a giant ant hill and reaching the Safari House hotel at 2 A.M. the next morning. We really appreciated this chance to bathe and wash our hair after Nondotto. We also picked up the bedrolls Tony said were cluttering up his office. Ansti told us we would be spending the next two weeks in the Serengeti National Park.

There were various mechanical delays to setting off—there were no towns or garages in the Serengeti, a park of 900 square miles. We were grateful for each extra day's delay, though Ansti must have chafed at keeping us housed and idle. From our point of view, we spent little time idle. We were taken out to the Trappe family farm one day, to look for rhino on the slopes of Mt. Meru another, to the movies two nights in a row, and out to supper with another game ranger, Logan Hughes, and his mistress. With Hughes' help we bought two leopard pelts, not very well cured, from the Game Department's confiscated skins as gifts for our unsuspecting parents. Mrs. Trappe's son said he'd cure them for us properly while we were in the Serengeti. I considered getting some Masai beadwork as a gift, but decided it would look unattractive on anyone but a Masai.

Oliver, hot on the trail of Prudence I supposed, turned up on our last day, just in time for supper with Hughes and the mistress. He invited us back to Mtu-wa-Mbu for the night on our way to the Serengeti.

In the Serengeti National Park

The last day of July we set off from Oliver's place. The road climbed up into the high land surrounding the famous Ngorongoro crater, an ancient caldera with a lake in its bottom and herds of zebra, gazelles, buffalo and ostrich feeding on the lush pasture. From the rim of the crater even a buffalo seemed the size of an ant. After passing the crater, we descended to the plains, stony and bare at that time of year, heading towards the famous Olduvai Gorge where Dr. Leakey had found the bones of Lucy, then the oldest *Homo sapiens* skeleton. I wanted to stop to look at this anthropologically hallowed place but Ansti refused. "Maybe later," he said vaguely, "or maybe not." In the States he had advised me to look up a Harvard palaeontologist "to see what we could do once the film is finished," but the palaeontologist had not encouraged any amateur scrabbling in this important place.

What I remember most about trundling across this dry sandy expanse was our initiation into Ansti's enthusiastic pursuit of "guineas"—guinea fowl. The shotgun was kept loaded in the cab of the power wagon, and at the sight of these birds whoever was driving had orders to skid to a stop so Ansti could leap out with the gun and run off into the bush after the birds. He nearly always got one, sometimes two, as they preferred running to flying. Should he have been shooting anything in a park? In the late afternoons we'd "make camp," search a long time for enough wood to build a fire, and set to work plucking these wiry birds and trying to cook them enough to get our teeth into the tough flesh. We got pretty dirty doing this, but could only wipe our hands with a wet rag. There was no water to be wasted on washing even the plates or pots, nor did we have any light after sunset to see by. In the mornings, we tried to clean the plates and pot with sand but Ansti, always impatient, threw everything into the chuck box just as it was. It took us two days to reach a place called Banagi, the Serengeti game ranger's station. We felt pretty bedraggled by the time we got there and Ansti was in a foul temper because his largest cine camera had broken down.

The game ranger was not at home. His staff, obviously under orders, refused even to let us use the verandah of his government bungalow to camp on. The clerk, however, took pity on us girls and said we could sleep in the office, a separate small building. As a headquarters, Banagi had a lot of resident Africans — scouts, boys, hangers-on, families — it would have been hard to for us to have to sleep in the open yard. Ansti, of course, had the truck. At least there was a *choo* (latrine) we could use, a fine double-holer in its own rondavel.

We stayed at this outpost another three days until the ranger turned up. We suggested camping some distance away but Ansti said he was sticking right there until he got hold of the ranger. He needed the ranger's permission to film in the park, and maybe also permission to shoot something bigger than guinea fowl to use as bait for lions. The

Serengeti was famous for its lions as well as, in season, for the migratory herds of ungulates they preyed on. We had already gone out every night to dazzle whatever we could find without waiting for permission. Towards evening of the third day we heard the noise of a land rover. We hid in the office. Let Ansti explain! The land rover stopped and we saw two young men got out of the front and a pile of boys from the back. We could hear the taller one shouting at the miserable clerk. "In my *office*! Why the *hell* did you let these people sleep in my *office?*" Prudence and I decided we wanted to die.

Ansti, of course, brazened it out and eventually we had to emerge, when it was clear we were hiding. It was excruciating. Ansti, greasy grey as usual, was demanding permits for this and that, while we, two sheepish girls, tried not to be noticed by the obviously angry ranger. His name, when we got around to introductions, was Andrew Bagnall; the man with him was Alan Salter, a wildlife biologist.

Andrew told me later that, yes, he had indeed been angry, but that when he saw us, he said he calmed down right away. Alan, who was only a guest himself, was polite from the start, but said little until he saw Andrew appear to accept the situation. He then observed quietly, "I'm sure these girls would like a bath," for which we blessed him, and the ranger, recovering his manners, said we might occupy his spare room if we liked and went off to see if there was anything for supper. He reappeared shortly with a rifle, got in the land rover again and drove off. Alan showed us the room, told the boys to move our things from the office and called the houseboy to prepare a bath. "Don't let it out when you've finished," he said. "We'll have it after you. There's not much water to spare here."

When the bath was said to be ready, we could see Alan was not exaggerating. In the bottom of the bathtub was a shallow puddle of dark brown water. It had been warmed, however, and a stub of candle had been stuck thoughtfully on bath's rim. Large moths flew in through the open window along with the cold evening air. Hurriedly we stripped and washed. Alan was next in. Ansti didn't bathe—he rarely did on safari, he said. He thought it more "soft living" I suppose. The ranger came back with a gazelle for supper and he got a little new water for his bath, being the boss, When he reappeared he was wearing a sarong and a loose wrapper. He called for beer.

Ansti explained the jungle night business and its requirements, in this case his idea of baiting lion, only he didn't have a game (only a bird) licence. He asked about places to go and the ranger suggested Klein's Camp, a place on the Grumetti River about half a day's drive to the north. He suggested leaving the unreliable Willys behind at Banagi, and said he would assign us a game scout and a boy to go with us. He would lend us a tent. He was still rather brusque and we thought he seemed anxious to be rid of us. Who could blame him? Alan had told us that all sorts of visitors simply pitched up at Banagi, like us, and that Andrew never liked it. "They think it's a damned rest house" was his usual grumble. We were the more embarrassed because Ansti appeared to take his hospitality for granted.

We thought about this camp on a river: wonderful. Enough

water to bathe and wash our clothes. We imagined something like Mtu-wa-Mbu. But the next day wore on without our reaching this paradise. Prudence, Kibiriti, the elderly "boy," and I were again riding on the back flap while Ansti drove, the game scout Kusheri beside him in the hot smelly cab. There was a track of sorts but Ansti kept leaving it to follow any

A tommy (Thomson's gazelle)

animal he saw, even though it was daytime and his crew exposed. The tsetse flies bit us viciously. I was side-swiped by a thorny branch which made my scalp bleed. Where was this place? The track disappeared as we got further and further into the bush. We began to think that Bagnall had planned to get rid of us permanently. But at last Kibiriti said, "*Campi ya Klini hapa*," and we drove into a clearing under some big acacia trees. There was plenty of space for tents, and shade to put them under, and some stones already collected for a fire place. It looked good, but where was the river?

The river? We had not got into our thick heads how serious the drought was in parts of Tanganyika this year. The upper Grumetti consisted of a trickle of water at the base of a rock, surrounded by animal tracks and mud smelling strongly of urine.

Kusheri and Kibiriti set up the tent; we had some tinned meat and crackers and went to bed. Ansti announced he wanted breakfast early: he was going to "scout around." There was a discussion about whether both boys would go with him or only one, but Kusheri insisted on staying with us on the implausible excuse that the Masai would surely cut our throats or wild animals would eat us if we were left alone. We all laughed. He'd probably had enough of Ansti or the truck or both, and he gained a peaceful morning. All he did was fetch water then watch with interest as we poked our boiling garments with a stick. We had no sooner hung them up on the tent ropes than Ansti reappeared and announced with more enthusiasm than he usually showed that we were moving camp *at once*. Cries of distress from us but we packed up and drove six jolting miles to another "river" which Kibiriti said was the Bolongonya. Once again the place was full of tracks and dung, but we had to agree there was more water. Ansti busied himself selecting a site for the fire, choosing we thought the largest pile of dung. "Zebra dung smells very sweet when it burns," he told us.

When it was time for Jungle Night, we set off down the track with Kibiriti in the cab and Kusheri on the back flap; I was driving; Ansti and Pru were on top. Somehow, as on many other nights, a lot of the animals failed to dazzle, and the ones that did dazzle didn't dazzle long. Ansti was also tempted into ordering useless chases across country after galagos (bush babies) whose glowing eyes in the light evoked the cry "carnivore" though they were high up in the trees. We saw only one hop-mouse, a creature we first encountered jungle nighting near Banagi. These small rodents, hopping on their hind legs with their front paws held up like miniature kangaroos, usually disappeared at once into their holes. I think it was this night that Ansti decided the small animal net was far too big and heavy for them and that Prudence and I should from now on run after them with a butterfly net.

The next morning Ansti complained he hadn't heard any lions at the Bolongonya the way he had at Klein's camp; so maybe Klein's camp was better after all. We said nothing. Our "kitchen" was exposed to the full sun all day long and the flies were terrible, but the shallow Bolongonya did have a lovely sandy bottom; and we were able to bathe. "Get one of these boys to wash my clothes too," said Ansti, looking at ours on the tent ropes. We didn't think this part of their duties, so we did them ourselves. Kusheri, we had found out, had been a former *major* in the East Africa Reserves: we couldn't ask him to wash clothes; and Kibiriti seemed very old. We had no notion of how strange this behaviour must have appeared to them.

I had just finished hanging up Ansti's clothes and Prudence was reading under a small tree when we heard the unexpected noise of a vehicle, still a long way off. It turned out to be Andrew Bagnall himself! We wondered that he could stand the sight of us so soon, and Prudence kept saying over and over that she couldn't "see what was in it for him here." "You didn't keep saying that when we were with Oliver," I finally pointed out. Bagnall even accepted the lunch we anxiously pressed on him, still trying to repay his hospitality, while Ansti lay on his camp bed in its daytime position outside the truck. The aura of a governor taking tea in a native hut prevailed until Bagnall took himself off (to Klein's Camp) *for his bath*, he said. His boys had probably spent the afternoon collecting the water for it. We invited him back for "dinner"— guinea fowl as usual.

Other People's safaris

This is as good a place as any to mention what other people thought necessary to take on safari—not just Americans who were rather unjustly derided for luxury items like iceboxes and feather beds. Tents, of course, with a fly sheet to sit under, a table and a chair (at least one of each), bed, bedding and a mosquito net, a canvas bath, warm clothing to change into after bathing, and adequate cooking equipment including several pots and *two* kettles, one for tea and one for cooking water, and as for food, eggs, vegetables and bread for the first days, a good assortment of tinned goods, cereals and bottled drinks. Well, we made do. We were good campers, American style. We were even a little vain about the efficient way we had learned to wash in tiny amounts of water and not complain about a lack of a toilet. There was all of Africa for this purpose.

Immediately on arrival at a camp (on a proper safari), the "boys" at once set up the tents, collect wood and prepare two fires. One is for the kitchen, the other is for the (bathed) ladies and gentlemen to sit around in their long trousers and mosquito boots and have a drink once the sun has gone down. In places like Klein's camp there was always plenty of dry wood lying around to make a fire, unlike the Serengeti plains. Ordinary safaris employ lots of boys, but even a game ranger is allowed quite a few on government salaries, so the life is very comfortable indeed.

Introducing Andrew to Jungle Nighting

The night Andrew arrived, we were without difficulty persuaded not to cook supper after all but to leave it to Andrew's cook, Muchoto, and to Ansti's annoyance the meal took place at a respectably late hour after a lot of gay chatter and beer. I thought Andrew handled Ansti rather better than Oliver, who was always trying to please him. Andrew just gave him a "I couldn't care less what you do" look.

We finally got off on a Jungle Night, Andrew's first. He chose to ride on top and manage the heavy spotlight with me while Pru drove, accompanied in the cab by Kibiriti, who had been woken from a peaceful slumber to go on this madness again. It was very cold and we were grateful for the extra sweaters Andrew lent us. Ansti sat behind us, staring blue-eyed at nothing. Of course it was Andrew who gave Pru driving directions, knowing the area. This was reasonable, but seemed to annoy Ansti. We drew blanks at several watering holes, but when a rhino and her calf appeared in the light Ansti came to life yelling loudly to Pru to "Follow, follow!" as the rhinos trotted off into the night. "That's never going to work," said Andrew undiplomatically. We'll have to bait if you want pictures of big game like lion. Nothing a lion likes better than a nice fat zebra." The idea was that this provender would so distract a large carnivore that it would ignore our lights, noisy machinery, human voices and human smell.

With Andrew there, Kibiriti and Kusheri, who had been barely surviving under our aegis, at last got the meat they had been craving (guinea fowl or tinned meat did not count) and Ansti, with his number two camera, would be sure to get some footage. On the way back to camp Andrew said he'd go out early the next morning with a game scout or two to shoot something. I was still in awe of this rather silent ranger, but I summoned up my courage to ask if we might come along. There was a slight hesitation, but he said "of course." He then told us, severely, that a departure at first light was essential if we wanted to find game, so I made a mental note to get up at five. Pru and I both wanted breakfast if we were to go off on some open-ended safari.

At five it seemed even colder; our clothes were damp, and the fire was out. The remains of last night's supper were still on the table, but there was a pot and a few reasonably clean cups left. Wrapped in our blankets we coaxed some twigs into a fire and made porridge. It was still dark at six when we decided to eat our share. There was no sign of Andrew, or Ansti. At six fifteen we ate Andrew's share. It began to get light and we were becoming quite peeved. We had only got back to camp at half past one that morning. When the sun had fully risen, Muchoto appeared and asked if we would like tea. We informed him icily that we had already eaten and asked for news (*habari*) of the

bwana. Muchoto permitted himself a smile. The *bwana*, he said, was just having *his* tea. Andrew was apparently greatly surprised when Muchoto reported back that we had already eaten and *didn't want tea*. He told us later that he never expected us to get up so early. When he appeared, he looked bright and well-rested.

The safari was not after all on foot but in the game department lorry (truck) and all the boys came too—all the game scouts, Kusheri, Kibiriti, Mrimi (Kibiriti's son), Mipaya, Raphael, and even Kindambo, the honey boy. Kindambo's main duty was to keep an eye out for honey birds waiting to lead men to hives. African bees are very fierce; and when men have driven the bees off and taken some of the honey, there is always lots left over for the birds. Kindambo was also the lookout for spring-breaking holes in the track, usually made by wart hogs, and for safe places to cross river beds, and was supposed to "fix" the truck engine if

Andrew

necessary when the "driver" was absent. The truck's official driver was a fat, good-natured fellow named Banana but Andrew preferred to do his own driving if only one vehicle was being used. Banana was therefore left in camp, sleeping peacefully. He had got his name, Andrew told us, for the easy good-natured way he had obtained bananas for the East African officers in Egypt during the war.

The game scouts swore there were buffalo nearby, but we didn't see any. A rhino charged the truck, veering off at the last minute. In the excitement I forgot to check which way it turned. Hours later, we returned, tired, with an antelope to eat but no lion bait, only to be greeted by Ansti furious to find he had been left "all alone" in camp all day. "I thought you were sleeping," he said accusingly in spite of the fact that our bedding was draped over the tent ropes. "We left you some porridge," we said, but he hadn't seen it. He said there were no girls and no food; there weren't even any boys.

After we'd eaten some tinned meat and crackers in the hot midday sun, Andrew said to me, ""Would you care to go for a walk?" I was very stiff from the long truck ride straddling the gear shift, and sunburned. No UV cream in those days. Prudence, being a brunette, never got burned. But I said yes, cautiously. Andrew disappeared. Pru and I agreed we ought to include Ansti. Ansti went off for his shotgun. Pru went to change her shoes (we'd given up wearing the hot boots). I put on some cream and a hat and Andrew returned. "Right," he said. "Are you ready?"

I explained about waiting for Ansti and Pru but he clearly did not want to wait. "They won't be long," I assured him, but he was already striding off. "We really ought to wait," I began again, but I could see he was not going to. I soon realised that this "walk" was not to be a getting-to-know-you stroll. Andrew led at about twice my usual pace and we were soon out of sight. I followed red in the face from heat and my burn, with Mipaya and Mrimi close behind me. We briskly crossed a dry river bed of deep sand and Andrew leapt up the boulders on the other side like a gazelle; I longed to stop to catch my breath but the scouts were right on my heels. We dropped into a valley, up another hill and then crossed another stream bed and up a fresh set of rocks. It felt like a mini commando course. I wondered if I were being tested, or if Andrew really enjoyed this sort of thing in the middle of an African day. He certainly seemed to.

We got back to camp about two. Andrew immediately put his feet up on the table (his favourite position when at rest), picked up The Times Weekly and started to read. There didn't seem to be anything to say, so I picked up a Manchester Guardian Weekly (said to be Alan's). Both papers were air mail editions several months old and once read were used for toilet paper. The heat was oppressive. I got bitten twice by the sneaky tsetses. They land on your skin so lightly you never feel them, then whammo, they dig in. Pru had taken a chair and placed it in the middle of the shallow Bolongonya to read her book where there were fewer flies. In a little while Ansti, deprived of a walk, lucky fellow, and apparently asleep on his camp bed, woke, heaved himself up, went to the power wagon, got his gun and wandered off. After guineas, I supposed.

I think it must have been this afternoon that Prudence and I decided to bathe in an ostrich egg. This egg had been presented to Pru that morning by Kibiriti, who had blown out the contents for her. The stuff smelled a bit fishy, but on the general idea of egg shampoo, we reasoned it must work. It did work, but we had to have a second wash after.

When it came time for Jungle Night, we discovered the battery of the power wagon was flat—Pru had left the ignition on from the night before—but we managed to start it by jerking it forward in gear until it started rolling down hill by itself. My turn to drive; Andrew managed the big light again. Once again we didn't see anything. After a while Andrew climbed down and took over the driving, giving me many blows from his elbow until he got used to the gear shift. The power wagon wasn't easy to drive. Andrew said he'd been on some unfortunate safaris, but this was the most unfortunate.

After two more days, when we had run out of basic supplies; he suggested going to a village called Loliondo and said we should go in his truck which, being lighter, would make better time. Once well away from Klein's camp and the Bolongonya, we saw lots of zebra and wildebeest, and every now and then the cry of *kanga* (guinea fowl) would be raised and Ansti would leap out and run off into the bush, hitching up his shorts as he went. We also got lost once, going twenty miles out of our way and ending up at the camp of a mining engineer named Kuenzler, a prospector of diamonds for Williamson's mines, of whom more later. Neither Andrew nor his game scouts had ever driven between the Grumetti and Loliondo before. He kept asking the boys, *"Sasa upenda gani?"* (What way do you like now?) Those on foot scouting ahead would each point in a different direction. It was beautiful country though, better watered, with high golden grass and big trees. We finally arrived at the duka about four in the afternoon. When the purchases had been collected, I asked Ansti for money to pay the bill but he wouldn't give me any. He said we always bought things he couldn't eat—though to be fair, Ansti, who claimed to have an ulcer, was very changeable about what he could or couldn't eat and we found it tricky to please him. A rather tense argument ensued in the duka's dusty yard. "Sympathy's a spark dying in the dark," he said loudly, turning away.

The tame Loliondo buffalo

But he had discovered, somehow, that the duka's owner had a tame buffalo and he now demanded that it be fetched. It was very old, but as I dashed past it on Ansti's orders, it did lower its head obligingly, so Ansti got a shot or two and eventually did pay for the groceries. I was determined that Andrew was not going to pay for our food as well as providing tents and boys. We paid for the beer. Our salary was mostly going on beer.

On the way back, in the dark, we fell into a serious hole in the middle of a muddy stream and it took us an hour to get the lorry out. No one had brought a flashlight. Everyone got covered with mud except Ansti, who merely remarked that we should have brought the power wagon, much the better vehicle. He was even more triumphant when after the second crossing the lorry's lights failed. Before we could find out what was wrong, a fire had to be built and automatically Andrew called for *chai* (tea) only to be told there wasn't any — news received in grim silence. Work had to proceed without it. Work for us consisted of orders to keep Ansti away from the platinum points, whatever they were, and to keep up a constant supply of burning twigs, soaked in petrol from the lorry's tank, to light up the investigation. The feed line and the carburettor were examined—nothing—but a vital screw was found to be unscrewed slightly and was at once blamed. Unfortunately the ordinarily nimble fingered Kindambo screwed it the wrong way and it fell off altogether into some recess and it took another hour and a staggering number of twigs to find it, and when all was in place, every time we went over a bump Kindambo had to climb down and make some delicate adjustment.

Soon after breakfast, Andrew took off after zebra. He marched off down the hill followed by Kusheri, Mrimi and Raphael carrying rifles just as Ansti appeared from behind the power wagon. "If one of you girls wants to go with him, you can," he said with a meaningful glance at me, "but one of you has to stay here. I may have some use for you and I don't want to be caught out." We hastily said we were both staying. "Well if you both go some place," Ansti continued, plaintively, "I don't see why I can't go too."

If we had been older, we might have been more sympathetic, even sorry for him. Here he was struggling to make a film on a tight budget and without luck, so far anyway. But his personal habits had become by now so off-putting and his attitude so difficult we were unable to see anything from his point of view. We just thought he should be grateful for all the free help he was getting, and make himself agreeable. Instead he just lay on his camp bed between meals talking to no one, or, if he suddenly thought of something he wanted to do, he'd rush off without a word. This day was no exception. After one of these bouts of activity he returned to say he'd seen a "swell place to take some publicity shots." He explained his idea of us dangling from vines above a watering hole. "Of course," he frowned, "it's poor publicity to give out the pictures and not get the story." He hesitated. Then he decided he wanted to use up the plates in his box camera anyway, and we were available, so off we went to his watering hole. I asked him if he preferred me in khaki pants or blue jeans (Pru was in jeans), and after a long pause, he answered "It's hard to say which I like better," which could have meant anything.

Ansti was really quite athletic for a man of his age—well, he was only 52 but seemed very old to us. He tested the vine's strength well before asking us to perform on it, As I approached this wobbly object from a fork in the tree, he told me just to walk down it and passed me what seemed to me little more than a piece of string to hold onto. I managed to "relax" on the vine, however, and smile, then Pru curved and smiled, and then we both stood in the muddy pool and smiled, and Pru held up imaginary objects, turning toward the camera with imaginary glee. I can't think what these pictures came out like. I asked Ansti once, months later, and he looked at me blankly. He said he didn't know what he'd done with the plates. "I just plumb forgot about them, I guess."

Towards the end of the photographic session, Kusheri appeared, solemn and military as always, to bring us all back to camp. Andrew had returned with a kongoni (a kind of antelope) which he wanted to string up in a tree as bait as soon as possible. Ansti decided I should go back with Kusheri; he and Pru would get the rope off the vine and follow. He gave the camera to Kusheri and I went ahead empty-handed, swinging my sun hat and feeling very *grande dame*.

Andrew was in his usual position in front of his tent, a place soon to be labelled sarcastically by Ansti as "the Night Club." By now we had moved back to Klein's camp. Ansti went off with the kongoni and some scouts to string it up. Lunch was being prepared by Muchoto I suppose, anyway not by us. All very enjoyable, and we felt that the morning had passed with more than usual dignity. This peaceful reverie was interrupted almost at once by the noisy arrival of Herr Kuenzler, the prospector, and his daughter in one land rover and Alan Salter in another. Andrew told me later that he'd left Banagi without telling Alan where he was going, even going so far as to take with him all the scouts who knew the track to this camp, so was not pleased to see Alan turn up here: Alan had given me quite a rush at Banagi. I knew nothing of Andrew's thoughts then, and was quite glad to see Alan. His sympathetic comments on my sunburn now, like his suggestion of a bath for us in Banagi, were pleasingly thoughtful. Furthermore, he immediately went to get some special cream of his own for me. Andrew had never commented on my burn one way or the other and I had concluded that either he'd never noticed, or thought I looked this way all the time; neither notion was very flattering.

Kuenzler was a round, fat Austrian with a round fat very nubile daughter about fourteen years old just out from Bayreuth, where she was being brought up by her grandmother. She was said to speak six languages and we were very impressed. They both wore very short shorts and told us they shared everything, rather improperly we thought from our vantage of seven extra years.

By the time the Kuenzlers left it was late afternoon and Alan said he had just enough light left to dissect the tommy (Thomson's gazelle) he'd shot on the way. Andrew wanted to go for another walk, but I said I'd rather watch the dissection and Pru followed me, leaving Andrew scowling (she said), smoking his pipe with his feet back up on the table again. Things picked up a little as the cocktail hour arrived and the sun "went below the yard arm." We had the usual argument about drinking before Jungle Night — not a good idea, considering the hazards. Instead, Pru and I had a bitterly cold bath in Andrew's safari bath.

Living Like a Pig

It was around this time that Ansti began to complain about "living like a pig" with all his belongings scattered "all over the ground." He didn't see why the scouts should have the little wattle hut while he had to sleep in the truck, etc. No one paid much attention, except Alan who quietly moved his things into Andrew's tent to forestall any attempt on Ansti's part to get in there. Ansti's personal habits repelled the men too.

Dinner was served in style with the aid of Alan's cook and his extra plates and we all piled onto the power wagon to initiate Alan into the rites of Jungle Night. By this time, Andrew was an old hand. He and Ansti entrenched themselves firmly on the mattress. I held onto an edge of the mattress with one hand and the six foot in diameter net with the other. Alan sat further back, and one of the guards took up a station on the tail gate. Pru drove accompanied by Kibiriti. Ansti looked a little alarmed at so many people, but we set off confidently enough to retrace his route to the kongoni. For the first half hour we fell into a lot of small holes but didn't find the kill, then everyone started to make suggestions, even those who had not been on the stringing up expedition. We came back to camp a couple of times and started out all over again. Ansti saw a pair of eyes he swore was a leopard and started shouting at Pru who was busy trying to follow Kibiriti's directions. There were frequent abrupt swerves. I nearly fell off a couple of times and Alan, from the back, called to Andrew, "For heaven's sake hold the poor girl on! Can't you see she's nearly falling off?" Andrew told me (much later) he'd thought that very generous of Alan.

We eventually gave up. Back at camp, we joined Andrew and Alan for a nightcap then trotted off to our tent. Ansti was puttering around indecisively. Alan told us the next morning that no sooner were they in their tent than Ansti's hand came through the flap followed by his head and a wild-eyed stare. Alan was standing in the middle of the tent in his shorts. "Say do you boys mind if I move in with you? It's just awful up there (their tent was downhill from the truck) — I live like a pig, you know..." He asked for help moving his bed. Alan said they'd already undressed and that he'd have to wake one of the boys to do it. The head and hand disappeared, a little disconsolately. They waited. Half an hour passed, then forty-five minutes. Still no Carapace. They went to sleep.

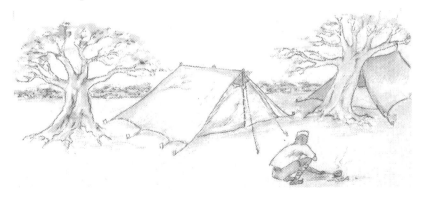

Camp – early morning

The next morning, hearing Ansti moving around, I got up to make him some breakfast. He always had porridge and a lot of toast if there was any bread. All seemed as usual—the bed in the truck and his clothes on the ground. When he'd eaten, he went off to find the kill with Kibiriti. It must have been well hidden because they were away all morning, and spent the afternoon blazing a trail to it. He had barely finished when Kibaya ran up and said there was a lion in the bushes above the camp. Would the *bwana* like to see? When this was translated from excited Swahili. Ansti rushed for his camera and the truck and said he'd need his assistants (us). I had to have a pee before being anyone's assistant, but behind each bush I chose there was a game scout looking for the lion. I finally found a place and was just squatting when I heard the power wagon coming straight at me. I finished quickly and leaped out—to Ansti's disappointment. No sooner was the lion chase over than another scout spotted an old male buffalo wandering between the trees in "orchard bush" in front of the camp. Andrew started stalking it and we followed him but Ansti kept trying to take shortcuts to get closer and was hissed at constantly. The buffalo paid no attention to all this and wandered off into dense thorn bush. All the scare stories about wild animal behavior that the old Africa hands delight in telling young girls fresh out from America never seemed to come true in our case. On the contrary, we were having a hard time even seeing big game.

That night we went straight to the kill. It was already smelly, but no lions were feeding. I was driving, Alan was in the cab, Andrew on top with Ansti and Pru. Alan chatted amiably in discreet whispers about his gazelle uteruses and gonads, while we watched the bait. Time was passing very slowly. There were a lot of thumps and bumps from the mattress-dwellers above. After a while a dark form appeared outside the cab trying to stifle her laughter: Prudence. She said Andrew and Ansti had both fallen asleep and were sleepily fighting for possession of the mattress. She made us all giggle. Then there was a bigger thump and Andrew appeared at the other window. A face white with anger announced its owner to be "leaving." He marched off into the night. It did not seem likely that he would walk all the way back to camp in the dark, but he did not come back. Eventually Ansti woke up to find he'd been deserted by his entire crew and decided we could all knock off for the night.

As we approached the camp fire we saw a figure with its feet on the table and stopped the truck at a safe distance. The radio on the table was blaring. He did not look up. Alan said to us, "Come on down for a nightcap," but we refused. Then thought we perhaps ought to return the sweaters and say goodnight. Alan turned the radio down as we arrived. Andrew said nothing but turned the radio back up. Then he said, "Have a drink," thrusting a bottle in our direction. We said goodnight into cold silence and went to bed unhappily.

In the morning, Andrew apologised, though we thought Alan must have put him up to it. Prudence said angrily that Andrew was just spoiled and selfish and I shouldn't pay any attention. I didn't know what to think. We decided it must be something to do with Anstruther, and that our role on this safari would probably always be to try to make up for his behavior, and to be humiliated by what others thought of him, and consequently of us. Andrew's announcement that he was leaving for Banagi right away and that Alan was going with him we accepted as the sign they'd both had enough of us and if they never saw any of us again it would be all right with them. Pru pointed out, gratuitously, how very much nicer Oliver had been with many of the same provocations.

Andrew did leave the rest of the case of beer behind, though, so we had some with lunch for consolation. Pru was depressed too. She was calculating how small her chances were of seeing Oliver again. Time for jungle night came around and we gloomily set off for the kongoni. There were a few terse arguments about who was to ride where. We all ended up in the cab, Ansti chewing his nails as usual. Nothing happened for two hours, Ansti fell asleep. We woke him when a very mangy old swaybacked lion turned up and he took some pictures. The next morning we found the kongoni had been eaten or dragged away and that even the valuable chain was gone, also a flashlight had somehow "rolled off" in the night. Kibiriti was kept busy all morning looking for these things. Kibiriti had been left behind with us, and, as a matter of fact, Muchoto too, but not Kusheri. Muchoto wasn't much use. The minute Andrew and Alan had left he complained of a serious *uma* (pain) that was *mbaya sana* (very bad); we gave him aspirin and he disappeared for the day. Then Kibiriti announced that he and Muchoto were out of *posho*.

This was critical. The question of meat was important, but posho (cornmeal) is the staple; life cannot continue without it. We began drawing on our cans of spaghetti and baked beans which they ate but told us they disliked. We didn't like them much either, but to us it was still food. Ansti didn't see there was anything he could do about the lack of posho; "Bagnall should have left more," was all he said. One more night, he announced, then we'd have to return to Banagi. Muchoto and Kibiriti cheered up at once, but we were apprehensive. Obviously we'd been expected to return Muchoto, Kibiriti and the tent sometime but we would have preferred not to show up so soon.

We left at seven in order to do another jungle night on the way. I wondered how we would ever find the track but Kibiriti was like a horse returning to his stable and never hesitated. Ansti and I rode on top, and Muchoto at Ansti's insistence rode on the tail gate to see nothing fell out. The stars were beautiful and lying on one's back on the mattress with the heavens rushing by overhead was exhilarating, though when Ansti took over the driving it became too dangerous. We finally stopped about twenty miles from Ikoma, a small settlement north of Banagi, at four in the morning. Muchoto was for once wonderful. He and Kibiriti must have been as tired as we were, but they got a fire going and helped us with our camp beds. We didn't bother with the tent. Ansti retired into the back of the truck and it seemed a bare moment before we were packing up again. We continued riding on top to Ikoma even though Pru said Ansti's driving made her nauseous; when we stopped, she retired behind a hedge to be sick. I felt fine though sleepy.

Ansti was soon surrounded by a crowd of people who all wanted a ride to Banagi. "Broken spring!" he kept shouting, "broken spring!" Ansti was quite good at mime, if only he wouldn't shout so at the same time. I stayed out of it, and practised leaning on my walking stick Masai fashion, and trying to play the musical instrument one of the little boys was playing. We got away finally but kept having to stop because Pru now had the trots. "I guess it doesn't bother her much," Ansti said unsympathetically, but in fact she became so uncomfortable that she was forced to ride in the cab with him.

At our insistence we stopped for "lunch" before reaching Banagi. We thought our welcome dubious enough without arriving at mealtime. Filthy dishes were dragged out by the long-suffering Muchoto and our last tin of Turi's Chicken and Ham Roll was found. It was already associated in our minds with hard times, but we were glad enough to have it. By now, after nearly a month in Africa, we had had chicken and ham roll with mayonnaise, with ketchup, fried for breakfast with eggs when we were lucky, and fried plain for lunch. Fried in gobs, or toasted delicately in thin slices, or mixed with other substances in stews for dinner. "Not even any Turi's Chicken and Ham Roll?" we'd ask a duka keeper when he'd finished telling us all he had. On this day we had it with what was left of the mayonnaise out of a filthy oil-covered jar all gritty around the top. In the full sun too: we had stopped in what Ansti called the cactus gardens, where there were only stark candelabra plants (a species of Euphorbia) and no shade.

At Banagi we were welcomed without apparent strain, given a beer and invited to curry lunch because it was Saturday. We were told that on Saturdays lunch was always very late so our protests about already having eaten were ignored. The minute Ansti left the room, we recounted our latest adventures with lots of laughter. The whole performance of jungle night had become ridiculous to us. Nothing ever seemed to work in Ansti's favor.

Eventually Andrew stood up and faced me uncertainly. "Would you care"—said elaborately casually to cover his nervousness, he told me later—"to join me in a little ride over to Seronera?" I hesitated. "Where is Seronera?" I asked. I was very tired and we had been offered beds for a nap. Beds with *sheets*. "Oh go with him, Wendy," said Alan. Andrew looked surprised but pleased. "All right," I said, feeling rather forward.

Little was said. Nothing in fact. We saw some lions and watched them for a while from the land rover. Andrew took photos of them with his Leica. He had a box with a great many different lenses in it and took his time choosing the right ones. Luckily the pride was very somnolent in the heat, even yawning, and hardly moved.

At Seronera a proper Rest Camp was being built for guests to stay in, and in charge of the work we found a young Kenyan called Peter Bramwell, known to the Africans as Bwana Maridadi. *Maridadi* means fancy or dressed up or flashy. He had bright blue eyes and long blond hair and was never at a loss for words in English or Swahili, and had always just had some harrowing adventure.

"Well, thanks for the tea, Peter," Andrew said. "You'll stop at Banagi tomorrow on your way to Musoma?" Musoma was a town on Lake Victoria forty miles to the west. It passed for the local metropolis.

"Right you are, Andrew…you'll be off now, will you? Well, cheery-bye Andrew. So long Wendy. Seen those lions up the road apiece? Nice lot, aren't they?"

We seemed to leave him still waffling.

Lionesses near Seronera

Bath-time at Banagi. How welcome the soft touch of the dark water that Pru had already bathed in was. After dinner, we guessed that plans were being hatched because Andrew and Alan began talking in Swahili. Ansti did not seem to notice, though Pru claimed he did. The two men kept it up even after Ansti had set up his camp bed right outside the open living room window. The idea was that if we were going to Musoma (much nearer than Arusha to re-supply) we could go in convoy with the Bramwell who could keep a lookout for the power wagon with its broken spring and the ever-ailing Willys. Then, after Musoma, why not meet up for a safari to the southern Serengeti where Andrew had to go anyway?

Another safari with Anstruther Carapace? We were amazed, but by now I had to admit that Andrew did seem interested in me in his silent way. Pru and I had even indulged in some girlish "what if" chatter about our, hers and my, possible future lives in Africa.

Ansti refused to consider any plan beyond going to Musoma. As there was no way of communicating with Banagi once we were in Musoma, we thought his brusque refusal unfortunate. Help was again being offered — boys, tents, guides all free and all was being brushed aside as of no importance. We decided he had after all been offended by the murmured Swahili.

Perhaps we ought to apologise to him? Andrew and Alan agreed. We thought it would soften his attitude. (Ever hopeful.)

Early the next morning I went to find him. "First of all," I began nervously, "I want to apologise for all the whispering last night—"

"Oh? I don't know what you mean."

"Well—I mean we were sort of talking about what we could do after Musoma, how it would be a good opportunity if the game ranger were going down a good lion area just now—well, that we could take advantage of his offer and plan to join up with him somewhere…"

"Well," said Ansti, "I don't want to spoil any of you girls' fun—"

"Oh Ansti, it isn't that. We think we need to take advantage of opportunities when they come up. It's not as if you ever stick around long enough to discuss anything."

Ansti stared at me blankly with those blue eyes. "I can't think of anything until I see what can be done about the power wagon and the jeep, and I would appreciate it if you girls would not go around making plans behind my back."

"But Ansti…" But he was already marching across the yard.

Muchoto came to tell me breakfast was ready. Ansti came in, evidently with a good deal left to say. He started with a bang. He was shaking.

"You girls," he shouted, eyes blazing, "have done nothing but plan this expedition the way you and your boyfriends want it ever since we came to Africa. You think because you're attractive to these men that you can boss me around, and that they think they can conduct the safari all the time where they like with no consideration for me. Look at the last two safaris to that place south of Arusha and this last place — I didn't get a *thing*, and you, Prudence, spent all your time with that game ranger down there!"

"I never spent any time with him that you wanted me for," she said hotly. "And it wasn't my fault he was kind enough to take you on safari—and he took you to good places—you just never have any patience!"

"And you were responsible for losing that net because—"

"I won't have you accuse me again of being so drunk I lost the net! Anyway, Oliver found it for you. We didn't have any more to drink than you did."

"I guess I'm a little more used to it than you are."

"I'm sick and tired of that lie, Anstruther, and..."

"Well, we won't discuss it any more now." Andrew and Alan could be heard approaching.

"We will too. I'd like to get this thing settled!" Pru, I had discovered, always liked to "have things out." And "get things settled."

But Ansti refused to talk about it in front of anyone else. We ate breakfast in a thick atmosphere.

Peter Bramwell turned up as promised and we prepared to leave. Andrew asked about The Plan. We said no. We gave some money to Kibiriti and Muchoto. Pru and I were to go first in the Willys. We heard Peter say, "God what a funny man! If I were those two girls I wouldn't let a man talk to me like that, I wouldn't!" Ansti had been officiously ordering us around.

Not far from Banagi the Willys broke down as expected, and had to be towed. At about 11 Ansti ordered lunch. Peter Bramwell stopped beside us.

"I think I'll be going on ahead of you folks for a bit, if you don't mind. I got to press on with this old buggy o' mine—she's not so perky these days. Mind you, I'll never be very far ahead. From the looks of your spring your wagon ought to hold up all right. Say, Mr. Carapace, can't I take one of your girls for you—or both of them? Seems a pity you all sitting in the front of that cab when I got plenty of room."

After a bit, Ansti said one of us might go but not both. If left alone, he said, he'd get "those left alone blues" again. "Yeah, and gimme that boy that's supposed to go with us to Musoma." Andrew had sent his junior clerk with Peter in case we wanted to stop overnight at a place called Chomliho or got lost or something.

The boy was transferred and Pru and I tossed to see who would go with Peter. We had to laugh at the fact that Ansti could never get away from men who wanted to take away his girls. I won and missed lunch because we set off at once, Peter waffling amiably about his family who were first settlers or anyway among them (these descendents of first settlers are almost as determined as the DAR), and about how the Jiluas, a lowland Kenya tribe, hated his folks because his grandfather had sent one of them up for stealing, and how he'd sworn vengeance and killed his grandfather and how the family murdered the thief in turn and so on, and how his mother had been raising tame pythons for years until one bit her, and about his adventures building the camp at Seronera and a how a beetle had "left 'is calling card" in his eye — "squirted 'is bloody juice in my eye, 'e did, on my way to Ngorongoro and I crawled in there after dark and when old Hewlett [the warden] came round the next morning to see what was keeping me from reporting, there was this huge red eye staring at him — why 'e backed out of that door so quick 'e fell over 'is own arse—pardon me, Wendy—rough life y'know."

Peter was known as a character. We even met up with his reputation later on in Kenya. He never went into the bush with less than two guns, and narrowly escaped death a dozen times a day, and at night there was always some animal "poking 'is bloody nose" into his tent. He had been narrowly missed by numerous puff adders — they had even bitten holes in the cuffs of his trousers...

Pretty soon we got so far ahead of Prudence and Ansti that we thought we had better wait for them, especially since Peter had driven right past Chomliho without noticing. So we stopped "to brew up a cup o' *chai*, eh Wendy?" I was all worn out around the ears by this time and very hungry and glad enough for Peter's tea and mouldy bread.

Prudence got stiffly off the top of the truck. "Oh I'm burnt to a cinder!" She did look strange, all dusty and heavy-lidded. We pushed on again. This time I drove the truck. Ansti took a turn on top to look after the Willys. To pass the time, I tried to converse with Muhanga (Christian name Jonathan), the junior clerk. For some reason, I was intent that day on learning as many Swahili phrases as possible. He finally asked me why I did not use the dictionary. I had just found out he had been brought up in a mission and that he was exactly my age when Ansti rapped on the roof. He wanted to come down to the cab. Then we "lost" the Willys going over a bridge and had to back up to rescue it. In silence we finally reached Musoma and its small hotel.

Pru and Peter had been there quite a while judging by the beer bottles. As I joined them; so did another Peter, Peter Kimber, a South

African, ex-elephant control and now in the crocodile business. His methods, he said proudly, were illegal but successful. We didn't believe him. He was fat and drink-sodden — he admitted to a bottle a night. He hadn't been to bed for days, he boasted. "Why don't you come out with me tomorrow?" Tales of narrow escapes from reptiles replaced stories of beetles. We parried by saying we'd ask "the boss."

We went to bed in thick sheets, but sheets even so, and under mosquito nets full of holes. Musoma was said to be a very bad "malarial area."

Everyone in the Musoma Hotel seemed to have been living there for months. At breakfast there was no conversation, only demands for the marmalade: one jar had to do the lot of us and it travelled slowly between the tables via the elderly waiter. The dining room, in the center of the ground floor, only received the daylight able to penetrate past the lounge and the corridors.

The town plan of Musoma was very simple. One road led out of town to the rest of Tanganyika, the other to the wharf where the lake steamer docked. There was a hospital, a post office, the hotel, two main stores and a collection of small Indian shops one of which claimed to be a drugstore. In a school some Indian girls were chanting their lessons but as we passed, they all rushed out to look at us. On a hill above the town was the Boma, a whitewashed low-walled fort housing the government offices, and at the very top of the Boma hill was something called Lucy's Folly, essentially a pile of rocks and stones in which the rock hyraxes had their burrows. Of all things, a concrete dance floor had been laid out near the Folly to celebrate, we were told, Queen Elizabeth's recent coronation. We climbed up to a bench near the dance floor and admired the view out over the lake, glad to get away from both Peters.

We had hardly been able to move in or out of the hotel without encountering one or another of them, and that afternoon they both turned up to "take us swimming" — though Peter Kimber said he was not going to ruin the effects of the brandy he'd already drunk by going into the water, and Peter Bramwell to our surprise claimed to be afraid of it. The lake was rather rough and choppy after the morning calm. We felt self-conscious taking off our outer clothing with those two just standing there. The water was murky, but we were swimming in an enclosure built to keep out the crocs and were safe enough. We walked back to the hotel along the beach which annoyed Peter Kimber who refused to remove his shoes. We had meanwhile decided we couldn't pass up a chance to go croc hunting even if it was with Peter Kimber, so we arranged a time to show up at the dock. We didn't tell Ansti. It was after all our free time.

As I was washing my hair, which was wet anyway, there was a loud bang on the door of our room. Pru, also undressed, put out her hand and a note was put into it. It was from Andrew Bagnall. Good heavens! The note said he would be "delighted to talk" to me if I could get out to meet him—he didn't dare come into the hotel in case Ansti thought it was part of some ghastly plot. By now we'd been in the hotel a whole day and had made friends with the hotel's very casual housekeeper, a jolly woman named Pearl who started on her own stimulants by 10 a.m. We explained to Pearl that we had to leave without being seen; and she led us crouching along the corridor past the lounge and smuggled us out through the bar creating no small stir.

Andrew said: "Wendy, my dear…"

"Andrew…hello!"

I was amazed at his coming all the way from Banagi. I was equally amazed at the "my dear." Wasn't it suddenly rather intimate? Or was it just a British expression, as in "Have some tea, my dear?"

We promptly invited him on the crocodile hunt, forgetting about Kimber's alleged illegal methods. In fact, Kimber was delighted and subsequently became a real nuisance to Andrew, pestering him for a game department job because he was "sick of crocs."

The night was cold and wet. We went down to the dock bundled in sweaters at about nine and didn't land again until the following morning, and as soon as were out on the lake it started to rain in earnest. Kimber explained his technique: find a croc, dazzle him with the battery-operated spotlight, kill the boat's motor, creep up silently and let the beast have it between the eyes. Easy, except he seemed to miss all the big ones and more often than not a dazzled croc would slip away with a slight swirl of water as we approached. There was quite a crowd of us in the boat, some of us whispering excitedly, which can't have helped. Usually none of us could see where the croc was except Kimber's rather sullen but efficient head boy whom he called "my eyes."

We returned as dawn was breaking over the lake in delicate pastel colors. It was very beautiful.

Andrew was staying at the District Officer's house, so we went there, wet and thinking about breakfast except for Kimber who threw himself on a sofa and passed out at once. The D.O. was away, Andrew didn't want to raid his supplies, and no shops were open yet, but we remembered that there were eggs in the Weak Sister, presently resting in the town's garage. Ansti had made us buy supplies, even fresh ones, before sending the Willys to be repaired in his usual curious way. Andrew knew the garage owner, so off we went, slipping into the hotel for some dry clothes on the way. At this hour we could be sure of not encountering Ansti. If our consciences had been completely clear, we would not have been worried. We even messed up our beds, just in case, and poured a little of the inky early morning tea into the bottom of two cups. We then drove to the garage, looted the car (no one even noticed us) and back to the D.O.'s house where we found his cook awake but no wood for the stove. We were all really hungry by now and Andrew told him he had to find some in a hurry and cook the eggs *upesi pesi sana*.

When we finally went back to the hotel, we came in through the bar again. Just as we got to the corridor where "cover" ended, we saw Ansti eating breakfast in a place with a full view of the door of our room. We backed up. I dropped the things in my hands. There were suppressed giggles. Pearl came along and in stage whispers we explained our predicament. She let us climb in through a back window.

We then collapsed on our beds.

Eventually we emerged as though very sleepy in our dressing gowns on the way to the bathroom, but this act was wasted as Ansti was no longer there.

Andrew had arranged to meet us later at the African-owned town bar, an interracial experiment that constituted the only center of night life in Musoma. It was a good effort and we thought there should be more ventures like this in East Africa. But tension in Kenya was high, and so many Mau Mau were rumoured to have moved into Tanganyika that the secret orders to government personnel to fraternize had been withdrawn. The Indians were also reluctant. Their aim seemed to be to keep African businesses down. Besides, Musoma was home to only a few European families — those of the D.C. and the D.O. and the Chief of Police and a construction engineer; there was also a house for the Nursing Sisters. All the other ex-pats lived in the hotel. It was pretty close quarters even for the Europeans to get along, let alone the other races.

We established ourselves at a table in the sweltering sun marked "reserved" and had got through a beer each by the time Andrew turned up. Then we had lunch somewhere and Pru went back to the hotel to sleep. I stayed and with Andrew and climbed Lucy's Folly again. I stayed out to "dinner" too. When I got back, I found Pru writing in our room. She said she'd told Ansti I had been invited to a party — good Pru — and all Ansti had said was "Oh?" So that was O.K., but as far as Andrew was concerned, I was mad as hell. He'd acted like a gawky schoolboy and I was very disillusioned. He was all of thirty years old after all! It was the first inkling I'd had that he was really *serious*, Oliver-type serious, and I remember being very disappointed to find him so gauche. I told Pru that I was going to have nothing more to do with him.

Meanwhile the plotting continued. It seemed that a Game Department "section" meeting had taken place in Banagi after we left, with Oliver and the head of the department (Gerry Swynnerton). They had consumed a lot of gin, disgusting the more refined Alan, but it proved informal enough for Andrew to slip away to Musoma. Oliver, stuck with Swynnerton, had to go back to Arusha with him. They all discussed the "Carapace safari" thoroughly and before Andrew left, Gerry decided to write an official letter to Anstruther telling him that from now on he was to be under strict Game Department surveillance. He had a copy made of this for us, Andrew told us, to save us the trouble of steaming Ansti's copy open.

It must have been this letter that made Ansti suddenly agree to the safari to the "lion area" to the south. The letter appeared to have been "sent by messenger" — somehow it was not linked directly to Andrew. Making the best of it, Ansti went to the post office and sent a telegram to Andrew in Banagi asking him to meet us at this place Chomliho and put a note under our door telling us we'd be leaving early the next day. We had an early breakfast and looked for Ansti. No sign of him in the hotel, but we found him at the garage in a crowd of interested Africans busy unloading the Willys, still not repaired. It was being abandoned again, in Musoma this time. In the middle of the street, and the crowd,

Ansti made us take all the food out of the well-packed boxes and put everything in that vile tin "chuck box."

The Southern Serengeti

As we left for the Serengeti again, we realised that Andrew might be seen arriving at Chomliho from the Musoma direction and not from Banagi, so we had to guide Ansti right past Chomliho before we officially "noticed the mistake" and turned Ansti around. We imagined we were getting rather good at this sort of thing. It was too bad Oliver couldn't join us, but Pru was consoled by getting a cryptic message from him; it was just my luck, she said, that it was "my turn" again.

"Don't worry," I said. "I don't feel very my turnish."

In the hot afternoon everyone but me went to sleep and I decided, bravado, no doubt, to climb Chomliho Hill by myself. I walked around the base of this large hill until I found a sort of track and climbed up until I came to a slab of rock with a wizened tree overhanging it, where I sat down to cool off. The view from the top, Andrew had said, was outstanding, but I thought it good already. There was a heat haze, but still I could see miles over the plain. I went on climbing. When the scattered rocks became boulders, I began to wonder if I'd taken a longer route than necessary but by now I was determined to reach the top.

Going down was a joy. I had never been a really good skier in the States, but I gave a good dry-shod imitation on the lower slopes. It started to drizzle, which felt wonderful, and I reached the rest house in time for — tea, of course. And after tea, Andrew said cheerfully, "let's climb Chomliho early tomorrow morning before we leave."

"I just have."

"Oh is that where you'd got to? You should have taken a game scout."

It started to rain properly.

In the evening we sat around, not saying much. We, Pru and I, were trying to indicate to Ansti that it was nothing to either of us that one of these game rangers was with us again. Andrew described the hordes of lions we would see lolling on the banks of rivers we would camp near in the southern Serengeti. I don't know if Ansti believed him. Later, without asking, Ansti moved his camp bed into our tiny rondavel which we thought very disagreeable of him.

We duly climbed Chomliho before breakfast, my least favorite time for healthy exertion, then packed up and left. I went with Andrew in his land rover at first, and Pru with Ansti. We agreed to change over at a place called Barata. In Barata, Andrew asked a scout we hadn't met before, Charles, who had friends in this outpost, to get some papayas for us, while we went to get some refreshment at Barata's "hotel," called the "Savoy." A large sign swinging in what breeze there was advertised cigarettes, sodas, comfortable chairs and doughnuts, among other things. We had some sodas and some doughnuts. The doughnuts were terrible. It was pleasant inside though; cool, with a packed earth floor, handmade stick furniture of the type sometimes seen in gardens, and a great number of amiable chickens, to whom we fed the doughnuts.

My turn to go with Ansti but we couldn't leave because Charles was still missing. Andrew thought Charles might be using papaya collecting as an excuse for dallying and drove back up the road to look for him. No Charles. Andrew had just about given him up when we saw him approaching from the other direction. He said the papayas were very bad at the end of the village where he had been left, so he'd had to walk all around the back of the village to find others, though the ones he brought were poor specimens too. Still, fruit of any sort was a treat.

I was driving the power wagon, pounding along in the dust from Andrew's lorry full of game scouts and boys, when to my joy I saw Andrew turn off the road and take off across the plains. Andrew drove fast, trying to make up for the time lost over the papayas I supposed, because we streamed over the dry ground as though on wings, quite a feat for the heavy wagon. Ansti claimed I took him on "quite a ride," and I suppose I did. I became exhilarated as one can do in Africa with open plains and no rutted track to bother with, and arrived at the camp flushed with excitement. Ansti said he had feared for both his truck and his ulcer.

The boys set up the tents and Andrew went to look at the river, the Mbalangeti. Dry! No game? No jungle night? Andrew apologised.

At dusk, to me: "Care to come for a walk?"

The dry river bed was strewn with the heavily scented and bearded borassus palm nuts, some half eaten by animals, and littered with big dry leaves. Along the river's banks the younger palm trunks were a mass of spikes; mature palms mercifully had their spikes further up, beyond the characteristic bulge in the trunk. We spent some time discussing these palms in an embarrassed way, avoiding what we were both thinking about. Suddenly, with a desperate expression on his face, Andrew's arm shot out like an uncoiled spring and hit me smartly on the shoulder. I jumped back into a spike. I said something stiff about not spoiling the safari. Andrew apologised, also stiffly, and we returned to camp. At least, we thought we were going back to the camp but Andrew's bush sense seemed to have deserted him. The Mbalangeti here was a mass of dried up rivulets and tributaries and there was no sign of a camp fire to guide us. As it got darker I was forced to accept Andrew's helping hand and had to admit I found his firm grip pleasant.

In camp, muttering about getting lost, we joined Ansti and Pru, sitting one either side of a dim lantern and waiting for their dinner. We had a silent meal. It wasn't much joy having Ansti as a companion, but I assured Pru later that I wasn't interested in Andrew. We went to bed cold and gloomy. Ansti was sure to be unhappy about the lack of lions.

The next day we pushed on further south. On the way, Andrew caught sight of a plume of smoke rising from yet another dry river bed. Poachers! He pulled the land rover around and drove back to his lorry bristling with excited game scouts in dusty blue sweaters and khaki shorts, We were too close to the poachers for concealment, so Andrew made straight for the fire, flying over the burnt landscape with Ansti bringing up the rear. As Andrew's lorry slewed into position, one of his scouts fell out of the back to shouts of laughter. No one paid much attention. The rest of the scouts rushed towards the poacher's camp, Andrew in the lead. The Game Department is not allowed to shoot first and the poachers were usually armed only with bows and arrows, but Andrew had thrust a gun in my hands telling me to "stay down." The game scouts had guns too, regarding bows and arrows as socially inferior weapons. Then there was a shot from a poacher and everyone started firing—I hoped over their heads. I caught a glimpse of Andrew streaking across the river bed to capture one of the poachers; the rest gave themselves up and the scouts trooped back to the lorry chattering excitedly with their prisoners.

Kibiriti had stayed behind to look after the fallen one: it was his son, Mrimi. The scouts, laughing again, mimed how Mrimi had just shot out of the lorry and fallen straight on his head. Mrimi lay on the ground, undoubtedly concussed. Kibiriti looked worried; no one knew what to do. "Africans are very tough," Andrew said. "Don't move him. We'll wait a little and see if he comes to."

We made camp where we were and after an hour, Andrew announced he was taking Mrimi back to the hospital in Musoma. "Have to go slowly. Don't know when I'll be back."

Ansti spent the afternoon, using his magenta lens for a night time effect, photographing Prudence hurling the net at various imaginary animals; towards evening he remarked on the roaring of lions he could hear "all around us." As we feared, a jungle night was ordered. Pru and I asked the boys still with us to build a really big fire to guide us back.

Drawing a poacher's bow

I was glad to be doing the driving instead of trying to hang on. We were in and out of river beds with steep banks for hours and it seemed to me going around in circles. I was so absorbed in the driving and trying to follow the instructions from the top that I ran over a baby duiker, or thought I had. Its mother had sensibly run off at our approach. We must have been a terrifying apparition with our big light and all the noise we made. Ansti insisted on going back to "net" the poor thing. It wasn't dead after all, just paralysed with fright. Pru threw the net as gently as she could and then ran out to "capture" her prize, still dazed. Ansti ordered her to bring it back to be photographed in the light, over our strenuous objections.

We saw no more game. Ansti and the Wa-Ikoma guide we'd brought with us argued constantly about which way to go; instructions were always prefaced by sharp bangs on the cab roof, very painful to the ears. I kept trying to see a fire as I drove over the endless dry river beds, but there was no fire to see even from the roof of the power wagon and the guide seemed lost too. The Wa-Ikoma, Kibiriti's tribe, are supposed to be good guides and are very popular with safari companies, but in the end we all spent the night on the ground, shivering with cold. Lions continued to roar around us. After using about fifty matches, a fire was lit producing lots of smoke and sparks but little heat.

In the morning we discovered the camp was quite close, though even in the daylight we had trouble finding it. Ansti claimed the boys had deliberately not lit any guide fire and we left him shouting at them and went to bed where we slept all morning. Andrew returned that evening, dirty and tired. Mrimi had died on the way to the hospital. This news put a pall on things and no one said much, just watched the shadows of the trees shifting in the firelight.

We pushed on in the next two days first to the Simuyu and then the Duma rivers, getting stuck frequently in dry river beds. Near the Simuyu, Andrew saw a wounded zebra staggering among the trees, the victim of a poacher's poisoned arrow. He shot it. The poachers had gone. Ansti decided we might as well use the zebra as lion bait so it was tied with an elaborate number of knots to the power wagon's tail flap. As zebras weigh about a thousand pounds the power wagon got stuck more frequently than ever. The southern Serengeti was beautiful country but arduous to drive in and the flies were terrible. After a long day we camped. The tents were soon up and beer on the table and fires lit when Andrew, gazing at an empty bit of acacia scrub hissed "poachers" and was off with such scouts as were lively enough to go with him. He seemed to be wearing seven league boots and it was a while before we caught up, to find him inspecting an elaborate poachers' camp. There was a well made blind of thorn bush constructed so that the lower branches of surrounding acacias both hid and supported it; behind this shelter, the ground was hollowed out and here we found lots of implements mostly of wood or bone and some cooking pots. Amulets hung from the branches. A cache of arrows lay behind a tree and a lot of meat was drying over a still warm fire. They must have seen us too and abandoned everything. Looking further, the game scouts found several carcases of wildebeest with only the tails missing. Wildebeest tails command a good price when made into fly switches for bigwigs and tourists and the poachers often do not bother with the meat if there is plenty of other game. Andrew said he never prosecuted a man who killed an animal for food, even in a national park, but these poaching gangs killed wastefully and on a commercial scale.

Further on, we made camp and hung the battered, smelly zebra up in a tree After Pru and Ansti had gone to bed, Andrew and I sat by the fire, a chance to relax without flies. I allowed my eyes to wander to Andrew's face and he smiled. Then my eyes refocused on the power wagon beyond him and met Ansti's eyes, staring hard at us.

Hanging up the zebra

There were certainly plenty of lions around, roaring during the night, and we found several lying up during the day easily enough. We decided to move the zebra which had been hung upwind of the camp; and in the evening drag it to a new location, laying a trail of strong scent no lion could resist, jungle nighting at the same time. It was Pru's turn to drive. Suddenly we all noticed an increase of weight at the back of the truck. Pru slowed down and I crawled back along the top of the cage to look down. There were four lionesses on the kill. The noise of the generator and the power wagon had ensured we'd heard nothing. Andrew called to Pru to speed up, to try to shake them off. Ansti was busy with his camera and ordering the spotlight turned around, and we were not keeping our voices down enough for Andrew who thought the lionesses could easily attack us. Fortunately they were so pleased with the zebra they did not bother, even with the spotlight on them.

"Net them, Wendy" Ansti shouted. "Net them!" "The hell she won't," said Andrew. Ansti ignored him, filming busily. I too thought annoying these ladies with a net was pretty stupid, particularly when I looked beyond them and saw three large males waiting their turn, but Ansti kept on shouting "net girl" at me and finally in a fury picked up the net himself and threw down on the lionesses before Andrew could stop him. With relief, we saw it land to one side, but unbelievably Ansti now ordered me to retrieve it. Andrew hissed, "she's doing no such thing," and Ansti shouted at him that an animal film was No Good unless something was being Done to the animals especially by a Young Girl and these were his orders and he was paying us to follow his orders. He was furious. After shouting some more, he climbed down, got in the cab pushing Pru aside and put his foot down on the accelerator. There were howls of protest from the rear, where the animals were keen to keep hold of their dinner, but eventually Ansti shook them off and after about five minutes had enough of a lead on them for Andrew to send a game scout down to cut the carcase free. In the lightened truck, Ansti now tore back to camp through the bush any old how, never mind the branches raking the crew on top, which now included Pru who said she wasn't staying in the cab the that madman. Just before the camp we came to another of those river beds and Andrew and I tightened our grip on something, but as we hurtled down the bank Pru just seemed to sail off the mattress into the night. Everyone started yelling and Ansti finally stopped halfway up the other bank. I was off in a flash and Andrew too and we met Pru on her feet and miraculously unhurt hurrying towards us. We were now all furious, refused to get back into or onto the power wagon and walked the short distance to camp where we found Ansti "sneaking" off to bed—in Andrew's tent at that, where he had placed his camp bed without asking. We called him back to "have things out" with him. Ansti had been very disagreeable to everyone for two days and the events of the night made us really fed up with him. But somehow it turned unto a vulgar brawl. Ansti, shaking with anger, paced up and down, accused Andrew of "keeping my girls up late drinking whole bottles of gin," making us too tired to work, of "necking" with me and a lot of other things. Pru burst into tears and I got so furious with his repeated allegations that I slapped him. This led to a fresh outburst: He yelled that I had "socked him in the kisser" (repeated several times). He then assured me he'd have no qualms hitting a girl back, so I'd better watch out! He seemed to take pleasure in using all these crude American expressions. Andrew told him no gentleman would ever do or say such a thing and Ansti shouted that Andrew wasn't a gentleman either and stood in front of him with his fists up, inviting him to come outside, barroom fashion. We were of course already outside.

Eventually we all simmered down. Pru went to bed and Andrew and I took a walk to a spot out of Ansti's spying range. A tree we had noticed during the day which had been smouldering within from some lightning strike, was now burning and we made for its warmth to have a good grumble about the behaviour of Anstruther Carapace. We sat as close to the tree as we dared. Occasional sparks fell at our feet. Andrew put his arm around me, more successfully this time, and I had just opened my mouth to take back all the things I had said at the Mbalangeti when Andrew suddenly threw me over backwards, off the log we'd been sitting on and onto the ground. I opened my mouth again to splutter when a large fiery branch crashed down inches from the log we'd been sitting on. I now found Andrew's arm very comforting; we joked about the possible expression on Anstruther's face should he have found our two bodies burnt to cinders — a suicide pact as a result of his insults?

The next day, driving back to Banagi, Ansti apologised to me, and we agreed to start all over again. "But you won't find me any different," he added, and so indeed we did not.

Time Off

Once back in Banagi, after a month of jungle-nighting, Pru and I asked Ansti for three days off-duty. Ansti asked what we were going to do with three days and we told him that all we wanted was a rest from constant camping and arguments. Whatever else we might do did not concern him. He looked at us suspiciously, at me in particular. He muttered about having to account for us to our mothers. We then revealed that we intended to spend the three days at Ngorongoro, the game-filled crater we had been whisked past with barely a peek over its rim. It was one of the most famous sights in East Africa. Ansti could not deny this, but was still suspicious because we made it clear that our idea of three days off meant three days without him around.

We arranged between us that Pru would cross the Serengeti with Ansti in the power wagon, taking the most direct route; I would follow with Andrew in his land rover. Pru and I would stop at Ngorongoro and Ansti would go on to Arusha to plan whatever he was going to do next. He had to admit there'd be nothing for us to do in Arusha over the weekend, only stay idle in the hotel at his expense. This way, the three days wouldn't cost him a penny. This was a powerful argument but Ansti insisted that he must have at least one girl with him or he'd get his "left all alone again blues." We brushed this aside. He could have Pru as far as Ngorongoro That was it. (Pru was presently in what we called "the royal favor.") Three days off was three days off. We had already agreed to leave without pay and were very firm. Ansti finally gave in.

Now the problem was how to delay him in Banagi long enough for our sub-plot to get Oliver to Ngorongoro to work? Radio messages had been sent but no answer received. Oliver might be anywhere. With anxiety we watched Ansti prepare for an early start the next day. Andrew said he could not possibly finish his paperwork in time to leave early. I could choose: wait overnight and, said with what seemed to me a very slight sneer, "to hell with my reputation," or pack into the hot cab with Pru and Ansti. Naturally we did not discuss this in front of Ansti.

I was in a quandary. In 1953 there were a lot more restrictions on a young girl's behavior than there are now. Nor was I feeling well. My period had descended on me, rather heavily; Pru and I found that this nearly always happened to one or another as we were about to set out for some long bumpy trip. The temptation to rest at Banagi was strong and not in the least romantic. Pru and I discussed the possibilities again. If only Ansti would go on alone, but he wouldn't. In the end we decided to hell with it and Pru and Ansti took off in the usual cloud of dust early the next day. Ansti never said a word, but I could see his mind ticking over with the letters he was going to write. Theoretically he did not know I would be spending the night alone with Andrew at Banagi. Andrew had diplomatically said he was just finishing his paperwork and that Ansti was welcome to wait until he had. When he left was up to him.

Pru told me Ansti never said a word to her all the way across the plains to Ngorongoro, where he left her, still suspicious but still in silence. When I joined her the next day in the little cabin she'd hired, we decided the silence was definitely ominous for the future, Stateside anyway.

And we certainly had a lot of fancy explaining to do when the letters from home started pouring in.

Meanwhile in Banagi, I retired to my room with cramps and a book while Andrew went back to his office. After a desultory lunch, more of the same. I felt depressed and out of sorts and was just dozing off when Muchoto banged on the door. Guess who had just turned up: the Bramble, the curly-haired wonder, on his way back to the Seronera. I groaned. Peter Bramwell constituted a one-man bush telegraph. I could imagine the story he'd tell, and augment. The bush telegraph was very efficient in East Africa and I could not hope that the Bramble's tales would not eventually reach Ansti. I wasn't much concerned with my reputation or lack of it in East Africa, only about the distorted version reaching home.

I got up to entertain Peter, very casual. I sent Muchoto to make a "cup o' chai" and to get the Bwana. Muchoto came back with the tea but no bwana. Andrew was evidently leaving me to it. I could just picture him saying "she'll just have to get on with it or we'll never get to Ngorongoro." I made some excuse for him by telling Peter how much "bumph" (a new word for me) Andrew had to get through before leaving. It must have seemed unlikely that anyone was going to leave for anywhere by this time in the day, but he smiled and said "yes," adding that he didn't mind waiting around because he had a little matter he'd just like to talk to the old Bwana about. So we sat there, and I buttered him up by getting him to tell me the story of the beetle-who-left-his-calling-card-in-my-eye again. He was well into the last lap of crawling across the Serengeti blinded by dust and beetle sting when Andrew sauntered in. I got no chance to hint that he should look anxious about time before he and the Bramble went off to discuss the thing of great importance.

They came back, both looking cross, and ordered more tea. When Peter was finally about to leave, my worst fears were confirmed when I heard Andrew promise to drop by Seronera on our way to Ngorongoro *in the morning.* Andrew told me later that Peter had met the power wagon peopled only by Carapace and one girl, and had just dropped by in Banagi for a "look-see," as he would have put it. The important thing he wanted to discuss was, Andrew said, some "footling" (another new word) administrative nonsense. Just an excuse, in other words.

In the morning, as we were leaving, Muchoto came wailing to Andrew to tell him his wife had run off with another man and what was he, Andrew, going to do about it? Andrew promptly gave him two weeks' leave to look for her, and for the Other Man. I asked what usually happened in such cases, and Andrew said nothing much happened to the wife, depending on the husband's clemency of course, but that many head of cattle were required from the abductor to pay for the offence. The arrangements were made by the elders of the tribe, the Wa-Ikoma in this case. I gathered that while the exact number, age and gender of the cattle to be paid were being settled, a vast quantity of *pombe,* (maize beer) was made and consumed, and that under its influence the business was conducted amicably enough. After such an incident, the husband has the right to give his wife away to some relative if he wants to, but usually she is taken back. After all, the injured husband is richer by a number of cattle, the Other Man is poorer and honor is satisfied. What happens if she continues to run away? I asked. Andrew thought she might be returned to her family and the bride price demanded back. Either way, the injured party would have more cattle. That was the important thing. I recounted to Andrew the frightful things done to unfaithful women among the Germanic tribes studied by Tacitus, but he observed that Africans in wife treatment as in everything else seemed to be much more easy-going than Europeans, even very early Europeans.

We decided, after calling at Seronera, that we were tired of the Naabi route, the "Lion Hill" route that Pru, Ansti and I had followed on our way to Banagi, so Andrew decided just to head straight across the plains for the purple mound of Ngorongoro. It was the dry season and the ground hard. Andrew called it "setting a course for the crater." There was something nautical about this vast sea of gravely sand masked by a billowy haze. The animals we saw were bodies without legs, gazelle shaped boats; a solitary wildebeest was a Grand Banker; a group of tommies clustered near a rocky outcrop were fishing smacks sheltering in the lee of an island on a foggy Scottish morning. Most of these poetical thoughts were Andrew's; I was concentrating on holding on. His driving was erratic but fast as always. It was therefore too late to stop when a belt of the dreaded cotton soil suddenly appeared across our bows, slightly blackish, like dry quicksand. Being better trained than I, Andrew should have seen it earlier, but he was busy with his poetry; and the game scout in the back was dozing peacefully as usual, though still able to keep a firm grip on some part of the vehicle. He hardly moved as we stopped abruptly with the stuff already up to our hub caps, except to open his eyes. We were stuck for an hour and a half, all of us crawling around collecting small stones to put under the wheels; there was no wood apart from a small piece one of us found to rest the jack on. Finally we found that some bit of the land rover could be got off and with that placed and replaced patiently under the rear wheels, we managed to back out.

We reached the Olduvai Gorge half an hour later and at my request made a detour to look down into it. A tree growing on the edge provided a small circle of shade. It was impressively deep. Embedded in the gorge's steep sides, eroded by a once powerful river, the skeleton of Lucy had been found, and I gazed at this barren scene with awe. Andrew at once, predictably, ordered Kusheri to rustle up some tea. Kusheri looked at him mournfully. "No wood." "Well, blast it, man," said Andrew in excellent Swahili, "find some!" In fact there was some further down into the gorge, but none lying around nearby. Kusheri disappeared and was gone a long time. When he came back he was holding a tiny bundle of the fibrous stuff Pru and I had used to try to cook our first guinea fowls, the stuff that never burns. With a flourish, Kusheri then played his trump card, "No matches," he said with finality. I think he was pleased to thwart the Bwana's absurd passion for tea in odd places.

At Ngorongoro

Crossly, Andrew got back behind the wheel and we reached Ngorongoro, dishevelled and out of sorts, at about four that afternoon. We looked for signs of Ansti or Pru but found none. Andrew suggested asking the Warden, so we walked up to his house. Both the house and the little camping huts rested in an oasis of green grass, very restful after the glare of the Serengeti and I said so to Mrs. Warden, who then told me at great length about the design and building of the huts while Andrew and the warden talked shop. Eventually Andrew asked about Pru and Carapace and was told the good news — that Carapace had gone on to Arusha and that the "other girl" was even now with Oliver. The warden, Mr. Hewlett, thought they'd gone to Lemagrut. Everyone then reminisced about some Game Department whoop-up until the Hewlett's son came in, diffidently. He brightened when he saw Andrew and asked at once when he could some to Banagi again. His parents pursed their lips and Andrew, having other immediate plans, was non-committal. Andrew told me, later, that he did not think the boy would be allowed in Banagi again: word had got back to Ngorongoro that Andrew had given the boy gin in his Horlicks (a powdered malted drink) every night "to jolly him up."

We got away eventually, feeling we needed some jollying ourselves. Andrew suddenly announced that thus day, August 25th, was his birthday, his thirty-first. I remember looking at him speculatively. I was twenty-one. Nine years' difference. He was very fit and active, but had already lost most of his hair. Did any of this matter? I liked him, and he had obviously given me to understand that he "cared" for me, but nothing definite had been said. I didn't want it to be either. I didn't want him to get to the point of proposing without having any idea what my answer would be. "I'll think about it" and "thank you for asking me" were both unsatisfactory and would make us nervous. Meanwhile, we could at least drink to the day.

As if the pop of a cork from a bottle served as some signal transmitted through the clear air of an African night, as I often thought it did, Oliver and Pru materialized to join the celebration. I don't remember if we ever got anything to eat, or where it came from. Oliver recounted having quite a lark trying to keep out of Anstruther's sight as they both neared Ngorongoro. He thought Ansti suspected something, but he believed he'd been successful. We would soon find out. We spent the evening looking down into the vast dark crater, using the telescope mounted outside the main lodge. We couldn't see much, and it was very cold. People don't think of Africa as a log cabin and blazing fire sort of place. I know my mother didn't from the amount of prickly heat powder I had been lugging around for the past two months, but the East African highlands have a lovely climate. I have been in some stew pots since and realise that it doesn't matter how hot you get during the day if you can cool off at night.

Later, .Pru and I discussed the age factor. We caught ourselves wondering, in an American way, what two such intelligent, presentable fellows were doing in such a low-key un-ambitious jobs as game rangers at the ages of 38 and 31, but decided we were being petty, or, worse, conventional.

The next day, we went our separate ways. Andrew elected to take the track to Nainokanoka (a Masai name meaning "place of heavy mists") and Embagai. It was a curious choice for a day's sightseeing in the crater highlands. The track is savage, wayward, humped, rutted and slippery. In general it follows the crater rim around to the side opposite the camp (very much in general) and thanks to the heavy mists we saw almost as little of the crater floor as we had at night, and the fierce jolting of the short wheel based land rover made even my "young" back ache horribly. Andrew had instructed me never to lean back in the seat, but on the return trip I kept flopping and the seat back would then immediately administer a resounding wallop to correct my lapse in posture. Needless to say we never made it all the way to Embagai and never saw the promised pink flamingos against the green wooded hills. We had a sleepy Masai "guide" with us, supposedly a Masai *moran* or young warrior, but he did nothing to keep Andrew on the best track and snored in the back most of the day, a miracle of agile sleeping at which Africans are so adept. At one point, on the downhill return trip, a sudden shaft of sunlight did light up the crater floor, illuminating a black rhino browsing among the zebra; then the vision was gone. The crater is so deep much of it lies in shadow most of the day.

Sporadically, by way of conversation, I asked Andrew to tell me about his parents and his home in England, and so on, in the line of finding out more about him and to vary my efforts to identify the trees and wildflowers until he finally said that although he was flattered by what he called my professional interest in his past, please couldn't we change the subject? He did not ask me anything in return, or suggest another subject; so we lapsed into silence. Now that I think about it, I don't believe he ever did ask me anything about my "previous" existence. I suppose he thought it unnecessary. Was it enough for him that I enjoyed being in Africa? I, on the other hand, was trying to feel my way into a life and mores foreign—wildly foreign—to an upbringing in New York City. In fact, I thought things were not going really well between us. Was Andrew aware of this? It was hard to tell. We had our baths then I joined Andrew in his cabin. There was no sign of Pru or Oliver. I had picked a lot of flowers but we could no longer see what they were because the cook, whom Andrew had acquired from somewhere, had the only lantern. There was no wood and no fire and everything was damp and cold, as was the food, somehow, when it turned up.

As soon as the food was cleared away, Andrew asked me to come to sit on his knee. Mercifully just at this moment there was knock on the door and a boy entered with the lantern and a few burning twigs with which he made a very small fire in the grate. This provided a diversion during which I realised I did not at all want to sit on Andrew's knee, though Andrew was undeterred. I first evaded then refused outright but in spite of this he chose this moment to propose to me, just as I'd feared. I said something about being a little more than fond of him but a great deal less than yes. He said "Oh." After that, we had a silent time of it. Where *were* Prudence and Oliver? I said goodnight and went to bed.

I got up very early the next morning and wandered around the main building looking at old magazines and admiring in a desultory way all the heads of game mounted on the walls. I then sat just outside the door in the warming sun until Andrew turned up. We had crackers and beer for breakfast, all we had with us. Andrew suggested descending into the crater, but I thought this would take too long and prevent our reaching Mto wa Mbu, where Pru and Oliver probably were, and then Arusha on this our last day off. We compromised by going part of the way down and back, which was warming enough, then went back to the lodge where I showed Andrew some of the comments I'd read in the visitors' book, such as "The earth is the Lord's and the fullness thereof," and "Why are there so many Masai in the crater?" and "Why not move the Crater and Camp to the U.S.A.," and such like.

About 10:30 we decided we'd better go, so we packed up and loaded the land rover and jounced off, taking with us someone begging for a lift to the bright lights of Arusha. On the way, I was much impressed by the loveliness of the land around Oldeani; apart from the Kenya highlands I had seen no place I liked better, from the point of view of farming, than those lovely fertile-looking rolling hills. But I knew nothing about Oldeani really, or farming for that matter, and Andrew could not supplement my knowledge much. It might have been absolute hell living there for all I knew. On the road to Mto I apologised to Andrew about asking him so many questions the day before He said the apology was "quite unnecessary." Silence. Then, on the spur of the moment, I told him some fairy story with a ghastly ending to amuse him and he laughed. We seemed to be on better terms now the proposal was out of the way.

When we got to Oliver's house, there was no sign of Oliver or Pru, but a boy woken from a sleep on the back porch said they were swimming in the river. We thought of following them but decided it would be more discreet to settle for a beer and wait for them to reappear. When they did, we asked them where they'd got to they told us they'd had a most exciting time. A game scout had told Oliver there was a herd of elephant near the hot springs at Maji na Moto on Lake Manyara, so instead of looking at the Crater they'd shot off there to make camp among the tall trees and, according to Pru, in the midst of an entire herd. Oliver was more cautious as to numbers. He'd also shot a wild pig, which his cook, Shauri, now produced for a late lunch served in a very Oliveresque way: in huge sandwiches of barely cooked boar with its dark hairy skin emerging from between thick wads of bread. Oliver then surprised us by calling for — fingerbowls! We could not imagine his having such things, but out they came and we teased him unmercifully, saying such dainty improvements were due solely to Pru's presence, which he denied. Full of semi-digested pork we then rushed off to Arusha which we reached seven minutes late for our six o'clock deadline. We imagined Ansti glaring at the clock, but there was no sign of him, and we found he'd gone off to Nairobi without leaving a message for us.

Relieved, we had dinner, played darts and talked. Logan Hughes appeared and told each of us severally and together about the affair he'd just ended and how he'd vowed to get hold of himself. It seemed we had another day off duty; Andrew said he'd collect me at some ungodly hour, to go to Moshi.

Arusha at this time was a hot, dusty town with two hotels. Moshi was also hot and dusty without any hotel but bigger, with a large messy-looking Greek church and several pubs of grade C variety. We went to a gun shop where Andrew spent at least an hour looking at things dear to his heart. We then tried a pub and went back to Arusha where Andrew dropped me at the hotel so he could to do some paperwork at Tangeru, the Game Department offices, to ease his conscience, he said. I went up to the room to wash my hair, the first chance since Musoma, and found Pru there with the same idea. We sent some clothes to the laundry too, wondering if we'd be here long enough to get them back.

There was a big party planned for the evening. We were to be collected by someone at four for a swim and the party would start as soon as possible after that. It was Oliver's "do." Oliver had commandeered someone's house to give it in, Oliver had had the chickens strangled, Oliver had requisitioned glasses and plates though he forgot the cutlery. Oliver was a great party man.

We were collected by Logan Hughes and the swimming was lovely. Neither Andrew nor Oliver turned up but Alan Salter was there. We got ducked a lot and Logan kept throwing himself off some logs tied to the bank and coming up with mud and leaves all over his face while Pru and I tried swinging out over the water on a rope and dropping off mid-lake at the end of its trajectory, scary but exciting. At the party house, there was food but no boys and still no Oliver or Andrew — just lots of people we'd never met. Pru and I set to washing lettuce and boiling eggs then cut up the chickens with the only knife. We had lots of help from attentive males and didn't spend much time wondering where "our" men had got to: we were terrible flirts, I fear. Finally while searching for a room to change out of my wet suit I found Andrew on a bed fast asleep. I started to tease him for his laziness but he just grunted and turned over. I was half piqued and half admiring. Propose to her one day, ignore her the next. Here was a man who was not going to let "love" interfere with his sleep.

He appeared an hour later to make some very strong punch with which he and lots of others got tight. Still no boys. Was all this well organised Bwana—boy business a myth? Pru and I cooked the chickens. In the middle of the evening, Oliver and Andrew had an arm- wrestling match on the floor. No one watched except us. We weren't as tight as they were and found the spectacle depressing. At one, the party started breaking up. Andrew took me back to the hotel driving wildly along the muddy road, scattering chickens in every direction — over the roof, even into the land rover. Why weren't these wretched birds roosting quietly somewhere, sound asleep? At a particularly violent swerve, I yelled at him to slow down. He looked offended and screeched to a halt. I thought it was going to be "you can walk from here!" but all he said was that he had to have a leak. "Five yards off the road at night, ten in daylight," he explained, and moved off, not very far.

I was asleep when Pru burst into the room in a fury. Oliver, she said, was both drunk and disgusting. She was never going to speak to him again! She flung herself into the bathroom and slammed the door. I went back to sleep. The urge to sleep was stronger than sympathy or curiosity.

In the morning, we found that Ansti had arrived at suppertime and demanded to know the whereabouts of his girls. The receptionist, our friend by this time, did not let us down. She told him we must be at the "fillums" and he had to be satisfied with that. He could see from the register that we'd arrived by the end of out time off. She sent a boy to our room in the morning with a note to warn us before we came down.

Ansti was eating breakfast when we turned up and joined him. He didn't say much except "How are you girls" and "I've been trying to think of something to do with you girls." This was calm enough. I don't know exactly what we were expecting, but our consciences were not entirely clear. Perhaps something like "I'm not going to pay your hotel bills for you to go out and get drunk with your boyfriends and be no good for expedition work in the morning," which became one of his favorites later on. Politely, with our best manners, we asked him if he did in fact have anything in mind for us this morning. He looked off across the dining room, cleared his throat twice, then and gave us another day off. We hoped Andrew and Oliver, if they turned up, would stay out of Ansti's sight. No point in rubbing his nose in their presence. But what about Oliver? Pru seemed to have forgotten her early morning rage; anyway she didn't mention it again.

Andrew took me to the Kibo Hotel, halfway up Mt.Kilimanjaro. There were a lot of climbers clunking around in spiked shoes, and guides waiting for their tourist parties. The tribesmen of this area are the enterprising coffee-growing Chaggas, who certainly know how to pose for pictures, judging by the hotel walls. We went for a slippery walk among their homesteads, but saw little as each was surrounded by a tall hedge in an unusually private manner for Africa; I suppose they were sick of staring tourists. Halfway back to Arusha we met Pru and Oliver on their way up. I suppose every girl who makes it this far from Nairobi is taken on a ritual visit to the Kibo Hotel and has suggested to her that, in the footsteps of Hemingway, she too might like to climb Kibo or Mawenzi, the sister peak of Kilimanjaro. Pru and I were no exception.

There was no sign of Ansti on our return, or that evening either. Trouble with his ulcer? Those left-all-alone-again blues? We hoped neither. There were dances in both hotels that night and we went to a film and then to both of them. The local belles were out in force with their political officers and insurance salesmen and the like. We did not see the gorgeous Tony but he was probably having a fast time in some other town. I discovered that Andrew was a terrible dancer but Oliver, though off-beat, was good. Not many men dance well, or maybe it is that the right kind of men don't dance well. (That had been my experience up to the age of twenty-one and a half and I've had no reason to change my mind since.)

August 30th dawned with two notes from Ansti under the door advising us of an early departure. We rushed to try to get our laundry back, pack, have breakfast then spent all morning waiting around while Ansti fiddled with the power wagon. The Weak Sister was still in Musoma. He made a lot of trips between the hotel and the parking lot with us at his heels, telling us about his latest idea, which was a real shocker. He was going to build a cage and lower us in it into the clear and photogenic waters of Mzima Springs, a famous tourist attraction in the nearby Tsavo National Park. One side of the cage was to be left open, so "if things got too bad" we could nip out and rise hastily to the surface. We were to wear our white Red Sea bathing suits and breathe through mask and hose, supplied with air by the compressor. We would thus get in training for the Red Sea and it was going to be wonderful for the film. When it got too late to leave, he gave us the rest of the day off.

The impression this idea made on our pet members of the Game Department was also wonderful. I don't know if they were more worried about us or the precious hippos in the equally precious springs, under threat from the demands for water from the surrounding sisal estates. It made a good story for me to tell Tony when he turned up just as Pru and Oliver were leaving for Tangeru. Tony said he was trying to recover from drinking six Pimms at lunchtime followed by an arduous round of golf. He was effortlessly charming and I relaxed in his undemanding company, laughing and chatting, until I saw him look with alarm at an approaching figure: Andrew, tall and serious, beers in hand. "I guess the Game Department has got you girls sewn up," he said with a wink. "I'd better remove myself before that chap coming toward us like a cruiser with an important rendez-vous can start getting jealous." I confess I was a little sorry.

"I'm taking you to dinner at the other hotel," Andrew announced firmly, looking at my safari clothes. "I'll be quite happy with a beer if you'd like to change."

I felt like saying "Sorry, but Tony's already asked me." What a beast I was! Instead I said "Thank you," and went upstairs.

The New Arusha Hotel was very cold. We saw the Ngorongoro warden and his wife there and they smiled benignly at us. Without saying yes to Andrew, were we already "settled?" This made me uneasy. Andrew was very attractive. I loved the life. But I did not feel in the least "settled." I looked at Andrew's kind but determined face and thought my unworthy thoughts.

On our return to Safari House, we sat for a while in the lounge, sure that Ansti would have already gone to bed, and watched the tourists newly arrived from Nairobi straggle in from their buses draped in cameras and other equipment followed by a great deal of luggage that I judged, with my two months' hardened eye, wouldn't last two minutes in the bush. Pru and I, on the other hand, had kept on shedding baggage, at the expense of a certain amount of chic, but it was worth not having to worry about the stuff. We were getting some letters from home, the result of photos sent, which said things like "you girls can't go around Africa looking like tramps" but we paid no attention. What did they know about Africa? Or even more, Africa with Anstruther Carapace and his greasy grimy power wagon? I felt beyond such considerations now. In spite of everything Ansti had said or done, I wasn't about to give up on the Carapace safari. I couldn't speak for Pru. She was less forgiving. But I intended to survive Ansti's crazier ideas and see the job through. I'd be leading a different life now if I hadn't.

Tsavo and the Springs

On the last day of August, we left early for Mzima Springs. Fortunately no cage had yet been built. Andrew and I had accomplished an extraordinary number of errands in Arusha the day before, without having a lot to say to each other. Andrew had stated his position and it was now up to me. We parted in a constrained manner, and I gathered Pru felt the same about Oliver. The two romances hovered ambiguously, unresolved. None of us knew whether chance, in the erratic guise of Anstruther Carapace, would ever again lead us into the orbit of the Tanganyika Game Department. Not if he could help it was our general assessment.

Squashed warmly into the cab of the power wagon, we drove off on the Arusha - Mombasa road to Voi, where Andrew assumed we'd be spending the night, then on to Mtito Andei, where we actually did spend the night. The hotel was very full, so the manager put Pru and me into the sewing room where we were given a candle; Ansti slept outside somewhere, we didn't care where. He had been particularly biting on the road about having "to keep you girls in a hotel," and to add to our gloom we had arrived after the time the management ceased to serve food. Ansti did offer to get out the chuck box, but we knew what the contents were and went to bed hungry and cross. Ansti had also refused to stop even for a moment for us to photograph anything, neither the vast sisal estates spread out on either side of the road with their orderly rows of spiky plants, nor the lovely sunset over the mountains surrounding Arusha. Who knew if we'd ever see Arusha again? It wasn't very logical to be cross about not stopping and about arriving too late for food, but there you are.

The Tsavo National Park is famous for its lions and elephants, but we did not see any, and Ansti, having come for the hippo had only hippo on his mind, so much so that he nearly drove into the closed park gates. Here he wrangled with the guard about paying the full entrance fee. He kept shouting "Only the hippo! Only the hippo!" The guard did not understand and remained adamant about money. When Ansti finally paid up he then refused to sign the guest book; maybe he thought it would commit him to something more. He told me to ask the guard the way to the warden's house and we received a series of instructions about rights and lefts and downhill and away from the sun, accompanied by lots of hand gestures. We all disagreed about the rights and lefts in the way of several people listening to directions especially in a foreign language with many gestures, but remembered the essentials about downhill and away from the sun, and so eventually got there. The warden received Ansti's letter of introduction politely, though silently, and even managed to keep any trace of the Colonial-Government-Confronted-With-Carapace look off his face. He never smiled once at us, either, which was a great disappointment, as by then we had become accustomed to our ability to raise a smile if not an actual laugh. I think this encounter must go down as the only cold reception we were *all* accorded in British East Africa.

The warden didn't even flinch at Ansti's proposal to lower us into Mzima Springs in a cage. He only looked at us with a tired expression and said that under no circumstances was he going to have his hippos annoyed. He gave the impression of one who had many troubles compared to which the imbecilities of the Carapace safari were insignificant. Or, alternatively, one to whom the then current fuss about using Mzima Springs as a water source had made the defence of the hippos in every respect imperative. We went away abashed.

Ansti took a longer route than usual to get from the warden's hot, dusty bungalow to the lush greenness of the springs in spite of the suggestions offered by our guide, a Park *askari* with rifle required by Park regulations to accompany us. At the springs, this fellow was sincerely tried by Ansti who was determined to evade him and immediately plunged off into the bushes leaving us to follow as we might. When Pru and I got to the pool, we saw the heads of two hippo at the far end, and Ansti, ignoring the guide's orders, went crashing off again to get a better look and find the best place for his cage idea. The hippo promptly went under and stayed down. Ansti waved his hands and gestured, for a stick I thought, but no one could hear him. So he made his way to the far side of the pool where there was more open ground, with us following laboriously over fallen trees behind him. We thought that the hippos might already be getting annoyed. Hippos, we'd been told, are easily annoyed, especially mother hippos, and had only to emerge from the water and come running at us with their big maws open and we'd be done for. It was a long way from my childhood memories of the fat sleek docile-looking animals in Central Park zoo, contentedly chewing grass and letting green slime drip through gaps in their large discoloured teeth.

Ansti drew no immediate conclusions, we gathered. He just told the guide in a rather threatening way that "We'll be back." We drove out of the park and back to the hotel where, by a miracle, we were allowed to have lunch before leaving for Nairobi. Lunch was delicious, though Ansti, who guzzled it with every sign of enjoyment, declared he'd rather have eaten out of the chuck box.

We left as soon as we'd finished. In the yard, Ansti backed into the shiny chrome radiator of a car belonging to a Mr. C. of the PWD (Public Works Department) who came rushing out, waving his napkin, demanding Ansti's name and so on and saying all sorts of unpleasant things. He looked like the type who'd get a new car out of you as soon as look at you. Since the damage was minor, we suggested Ansti get out with lots of promises and as little as possible on paper, but we could have kept our mouths shut. Ansti was an old hand at that game. His only comment for the next two miles was that he really must replace the (external) rear view mirror, the one that had been lost bush-whacking and miraculously found by Oliver's game scouts. We finally stopped to do this, hunting for the tools in the back and then with a lot of instructions from Ansti about the angle and re-bending the stem and irritated comments between us about who had what screw. All this took place in lovely country with those deceptively soft-looking acacias and beautiful birds flying up from the roadside. Whatever the reason, we were glad to get out of the cab and away from Ansti who was smelling high from his morning exertions.

We crossed the stony Athi after arguing Ansti out of taking an indistinctly marked turning to Machakos just as the Kapiti plains were losing their harsh outlines in a covering of blackish purple shadows. I was driving by this time. Ansti was worried about getting into Nairobi before the road block closed to incoming cars (an anti Mau Mau measure) and kept nagging me to drive faster. We made Nairobi by seven and Ansti put us all in the Avenue Hotel again, having discovered it to be the cheapest. We had a gloomy dinner. "I wish K [my mother] were here," Ansti kept saying. We didn't ask why.

We spent the next five days in Nairobi in a fever of uncertainty. On the fourth day, Prudence wrote home saying "It has come to pass that our employment may terminate at a moment's notice," and that she will "reveal" the reasons in her next letter (a habit of hers) but that the "more important ones are that permission to do night photography have not been forthcoming, and that Mr. Carapace now thought that the light for the film he'd already taken might not have been strong enough… so he might not have any more use for us in which case Wendy and I have decided to get jobs. We are not worried at all. There is a great demand for intelligent girls here and we have many friends who will help us. We could of course go home, but Mr. Carapace still wants us later for the Red Sea for work in November and December, and besides we now love Africa and want to stay here by hook or crook, six months anyway, if possible." Prudence was smart. A good outline of the situation, but a long way from the full story.

Still, no one could have given all the reasons for Ansti's frequent but intermittent desire to fire us, matched by our sporadic desire to leave him. These bust-ups always happened when Ansti felt he was no longer the boss, usually when another man was showing up his incompetence. The other man business was tricky to explain to our parents, but some sort of explanation had to go off home. Interrupted frequently either by being temporarily fired, or by being told we weren't fired and were leaving Nairobi the very next moment, Pru and I wrote and wrote.

Nairobi, 4th September
Dear Mother

Latest bulletin: we definitely leave tomorrow—naturally just as I have managed to get an appointment with the great Leakey for tomorrow morning. But I put it to Ansti that if he was going to give us notice every

Prudence

day, the least he could do was to realise we had to find another job, so tomorrow we are *all* going to the Coryndon Museum for my appointment. I hope Ansti will restrain himself from rushing in on any of the people there. The entire Game and Fisheries Department inhabits various parts of this museum and is thus vulnerable.

I imagine you have already received an ill-tempered letter from the Boss with a roster of complaints about our immoral activities with Game Rangers and a long list of the names I have called him. He said he was going to send this list, and that you would surely be on his side. I regret to say our time in the Serengeti was the scene and in some ways the cause of many a fight with Ansti in spite of all our resolves. Just occasionally he has to be prevented from killing us and himself, but he reacts badly to such interference. Then there are his personal habits: he is rude, smells bad and eats like a pig. In towns, his manners are a little better, but not much.

I hope you do not think we are being unreasonable without extreme provocation. We know he is not fully responsible for what he does and says. But though we have often sat silently and passively letting him change his mind 19 times in an hour (we counted once), the best decision for the expedition is always so obvious we can't keep our mouths shut for long. Nor are we so perfect that we are immune to offers of help. Ansti may insist that he operates better by himself, but he would never have gone to or even known about the places we've been shown by the Game Department of Tanganyika; indeed everyone tells us frankly that he only gets all this help because we are with him. But instead of being grateful he is angry and suspicious.

He says he's trying to get hold of that "champ swimmer" from Hollywood, by the way. If she's foolish enough to come out here, we, who are foolish enough to want to stay on, go. But I'll bet she won't last long. We manage because there are two of us (and Ansti is even jealous of this fact, apparently). From her photos, this champ swimmer is quite a dish and thus bound to be more exacting than we are. He likes her looks a lot and tonight told us that although an employer shouldn't flirt with an employee, if he did, the employee had no right to say nasty things to him, and if she did, he had every right to fire her and get another. "One more satisfactory? asked Pru brightly. But Ansti slid off the subject.

I must stop—still without being able to tell you where we are going…. If Ansti should let us go now and Mr. Leakey does not offer me anything tomorrow, I suppose we could get some sort of teaching jobs either here in Nairobi or in Mombasa. Mombasa is a nice place, apparently, and we could hop up to Malindi for some goggling with this or that set of friends we plan on meeting. And as for the Game Rangers, please don't go by what Ansti says about our relations with them, though it's true that I spent a night unchaperoned with Andrew at Banagi Hill, and that Pru and I both stayed at the Ngorongoro Rest Camp with them (but in our own cabin), and that Pru spent another night out on safari near Maji Moto (hot springs) on Lake Manyara. Ansti is convinced of the worst, of course, and I notice that there have been no more remarks to me since about my supposed blue-blooded aristocraticness.

As of this moment, it looks as though Ansti will want us for a month anyway. Much depends on this other girl. She's better looking than we are, and will no doubt be better for the picture than our two lumpy forms in borrowed sweaters bobbing in and out of the Jungle Night spotlight.

We Go to Loliondo (again)

In the morning, early, by chance we met the hotel detective on the street outside the hotel. He was a greasy-looking man in a loud tweed suit, but brainy. He winked at us, and told us "all Arusha" was in town. We flew into a panic at once. But the only one we saw was Logan Hughes, and that a long way off. He didn't see us, and we didn't dare to do much looking around for "Arusha" because we were anxious to avoid the persistent Ahmed. At college, Ahmed had never given me a glance, but here he seemed very anxious to prove to his friends how accustomed he was to dating white girls. The last double date had been dire: a painful meal then a cruise along a ridge outside Nairobi looking at the city's lights. Pru claimed to have been pinched by the fat lawyer friend while I sat in front with Ahmed, who kept his hands on the wheel.

By the time Ansti had done all his errands and the power wagon was loaded, I could see I was going to be late for my appointment, but we rolled up to the museum only five minutes behind time. Leakey did not say either yes or no to a job, exactly, only that there was little or no money to pay me. A bird expert I met on the way out said this was vaguely promising, but I told him I really did need a salary however small. The bird man, a small neat person, said he knew the head of the East African Women's League, and when we came back to Nairobi, he would introduce me. This was very kind, and I left the museum encouraged. As soon as I got back in the cab of the truck, we roared off on the Rift Valley road: Ansti, after much nail-chewing, had decided not to collect the station wagon in Musoma after all but instead to go to Thomson's Falls and Carr Hartley's game ranch. He was tired, he said, of driving around the bush trying to photograph recalcitrant animals or, worse, seeing nothing (except game rangers), but the decision was a painful one. Carr Hartley charged good money to photograph his animals, and Ansti already thought he was getting a poor return.

Just before the Kikuyu Reserve, I opened my mouth to say something or other when the truck gave a kind of gasp and then rolled to a gentle and silent halt. "My God," said Ansti, "we're out of gas! Glad you noticed, Wendy—don't know what we'd do without you!" I opened my mouth again but shut it promptly. There was little enough to our credit so far.

A passer-by gave us some fuel (Africa is like that) and we continued to Thomson's Falls and Carr Hartley's place but didn't stay. Ansti hadn't booked ahead, they were full up and hadn't room for us, so we went back to Nairobi, back to the Avenue Hotel and were again put on daily departure notice, to somewhere. Daily we dressed in safari clothes and packed our bags; daily the room boys took away our sheets and cleaned the room, but we never actually left. "Reception" got very annoyed with us. At the Embassy I found a long letter from Andrew asking for our plans (!) and saying that he and Oliver wanted to take us on an elephant hunt before we got other jobs. The letter had been written while he was on safari around the Mara and Grumetti rivers and was full of closely written descriptions of the scenery in the various places he'd been. Digested slowly, it was very interesting if rather impersonal. I remember feeling I had turned on a tap by removing my presence and leaving him with paper and a pen for company. The letter was addressed

"Dearest Wendy" which I thought a bit forward of him, forgetting that Andrew was not troubled by my uncertainties.

I think we spent three days getting ready to go somewhere before we actually left and Ansti only announced our destination once he had us and everything else in the truck: we were going back south after all, back to Loliondo to photograph the tame buffalo, camping on the way. "But we have no food," we objected. "Why didn't you tell us?" He ignored us stoically, quite a feat in the close confines of the power wagon's cab.

We set course for Narok on the Kenya-Tanganyika border, apparently looking for some white hunter he thought was there. He wasn't but the D.C. gave us some directions and Ansti let us buy food, to which we added some beer, separately paid for by us, though Ansti thought he was paying for it so there was a row. The directions also disappeared in arguments and we soon found ourselves bumping over open country with only the sun to guide us. Towards evening we camped and Ansti discovered he'd had left the water supply behind in Narok. Fortunately we had tinned soup, and we shared our beer with him for which we got no thanks. "Tastes soapy," he said.

I still remember the place where we camped, a gently sloping hillside covered with yellow grass and dotted with stunted trees like olives, their foliage so deep a green (in the twilight) as to look almost black. It was drizzling, but there was plenty of dry wood for a fire and we settled into our bed rolls happily enough. I had a small flashlight and a book, lent me by Andrew, called *Cage Me a Peacock*. It made me laugh at almost every other sentence. Pru said this was very annoying.

In the morning there was a debate about whether or not to go on to Loliondo without water, supposing we could find the place. We had a map, but only a vague notion of where we were on it, and the map showed plenty of streams, though they might be dry. For once no one wanted to make the decision. For breakfast we had tinned peaches and toasted Ryvita, all of us moving around the fire to keep warm and out of the smoke. It started to rain, which seemed to settle the water question.

We packed up, always a testing time, and moved off downhill, we hoped towards Loliondo, bumping over miles of a rock-strewn track slippery with mud from the rain, now falling steadily. I said, "Perhaps someone has died today." It seemed that sort of day. The windshield wiper fell off twice. We stopped several times for Ansti to relieve himself. He said he had the trots.

In Loliondo, Ansti couldn't decide whether to see the District Officer first or go to the duka where the buffalo was. Twice we turned around. Finally he settled on the duka, only to find the buffalo was dead.

It was a times like this that even we thought the expedition fated. We seemed to be bucking impossible odds. Still, if Ansti was persevering, so were we, and as soon as he went off to see the D.O., we rushed to the post office to send telegrams to the rangers. Unfortunately Ansti came back before us, and found out where we'd gone, his wits sharpened by adversity. There was another disagreeable scene. We then returned to the duka where the proprietors invited us for tea, after which they said they'd give us a guide to show us the way to the government rest house: Loliondo was a surprisingly large and spread out village.

Ansti, who claimed we had arranged and accepted this invitation to tea totally without his knowledge or agreement, sullenly joined us the Djillon's living quarters in the back of the shop. We did our best to ignore him. The duka was a real general store, Indian-style, with bins of sugar, flour, rice and *posho*, bolts of cloth, the usual British tinned foods, piles of pails and cooking pots, tin plates and mugs and shelves of mysterious herbal medicines like Extract of Male Fern. Some of the plates and mugs were especially colourful with badly applied red, blue and orange flowers. These were very popular with the Masai hanging around and were being much fingered. There were lots of Masai in the outer store and in the yard, fingering things. Mrs. Djillon had a deep-seated distrust of the Masai, probably well-founded, for there was a good deal of jumping up from the tea table and excited injunctions when they became too bold. She told us she and Mr. Djillon had been in Loliondo fourteen years and they had five children and that Mr. Djillon made the trip to Nairobi to re-supply every two weeks, even in the rainy season. She indicated a vintage truck. We were in a good position to appreciate his fortitude and devotion to his business.

The Masai were obviously "in town" in force for some reason, and Mrs. Djillon told us with a pained expression on her pretty face that it was cattle auction time, and that all the Masai for miles around were gathered to sell their stock to the English and Indian buyers. She said it was a time of much trouble for her.

During this conversation, Ansti sat staring at the pink pictures on the pink walls of her small parlour and eating away steadily at her biscuits. Whenever he spoke, he spoke in an accent we had never heard him use before, a sort of bad parody of Mrs. Djillon's own. We thought it the worst sort of ill manners and tried to ensure there were few gaps in the conversation for him to fill. He stopped fidgeting, and eating, however, when Mrs. Djillon suddenly revealed that her husband in addition to all his business duties was also an (Indian) White Hunter. He said nothing but this revelation had clearly made an impression on him.

After the Djillons', the rest house was cold and bleak. A normal safari would have had boys to provide firewood and water but Mr. Djillon's guide did none of these things and stared blankly at us when we asked where and how they were to be obtained. The rest house was quite a long way from Mr. Djillon's duka and when Ansti refused to take him back to the duka in the truck, he disappeared and was not seen again.

Ansti spent the rest of the afternoon brooding. This was never a good sign. Just before supper he made in our direction with Something to Say. "It's my business," he announced, "to tell government officials of our whereabouts. I won't have you girls sending off telegrams to your boyfriends about where to meet you," and more of the same. After rejecting several possible replies on the grounds that Ansti did have a point, I said mildly that it really was our business what we wrote to our friends, but Pru added, hotly, "Perhaps you should censor our letters too!" A trapped animal look crossed Ansti's face and he made off. We were pretty awful sometimes, but the ill feeling was mutual and each side felt driven to confrontation by the other.

In this mood, we went jungle-nighting and the object of that night's search was the infamous hop-mouse. It was my turn to drive, but both Pru and I were made to do a great deal of running round over ankle-twisting tussocks after these wretched animals, whose ability to find a hole when one is almost on them I think I have mentioned before. I rather enjoyed the challenge, in a perverse way, but Pru had been feeling out of sorts all day and running after hop-mice did not improve her temper. Still, there were certain things to be thankful for. We had a roof over our heads. It was a blessing to be able to get water even though we had to lug it up from a small spring, and it was a blessing just to be able to shut a door on Ansti even though it was only a door in a rough partition. In addition we were near a store, and a post office. Loliondo also proved to have a prison, a dispensary, a Lutheran mission and a school; it was practically a real town.

It was definitely not among our blessings that Pru and I were beginning to quarrel with each other. The uncertainty of our life, which I enjoyed, got her down. She couldn't see why Ansti could not make up his mind to do something and then do it. I might be willing just to float along, but it was driving her crazy, she told me, and I thought from her expression that probably both Ansti and I were driving her crazy equally, which I guess was true.

On the way back to the rest house after a final hop-mouse attempt, Ansti said in a toneless voice that a beer might be nice. Beer! A loaded word. He got a glassful, but rather stiffly.

The next two days we all sat in the cold rest house because the rain, early for the small rains, poured out of the sky without stopping except very briefly around midday. Why were we spending so much time in Loliondo? Ansti would not tell us. We decided that either he did not know himself, or that he was keeping any plan he had secret so we would not tell our boyfriends. Anyway, it gave us time to catch up on our diaries and letters home. We had pretty good meals too, with a stove to cook on, and even coffee for breakfast. I decided that since there was a table I'd unearth my small portable typewriter from the bowels of the truck and use it, only to find it broken. Our clothes and bedding rolls had been soaked in fuel or covered in oil and my camera broken, but so far the typewriter had survived, and now we were 150 miles away from any chance to repair it. Then I had an idea. Mr. Djillon could take it to Nairobi on his next trip. I broached this idea with Ansti.

"He's not going," Ansti said flatly.

"Why not? He goes every two weeks. He must be nearly ready to go now."

"He's not going because he's coming with us."

It turned out that what we were doing was waiting for Mr. Djillon to put his affairs in order so that he could take us into the bush as our White Hunter. Ansti had actually hired a white hunter! But Mr. Djillon was of a cautious nature and obviously thought going into the bush required very careful preparation. During a visit to his shop, I made some comment about the ease with which game rangers went on safari, but he silenced me quickly. "Yes," he said, "but man, you know they live like dogs or wild beasts in the bush."

I tried to get on with my diary well into the evenings, interrupted constantly by Ansti who kept going to bed and then getting up again. He drank one of our beers, and then went out, only to pop back in holding a bottle of whiskey, which was unusual for him. "Can I tempt you?" he asked. I refused politely, and he poured himself a drink. Funnily enough, strained relations between Ansti and me seemed less noticeable when Pru was out of the room. By now she hated Ansti so much the atmosphere was stirred up to a terrible pitch whenever she was around, cooped up as we were by the rain. Ansti left with the whisky but ten minutes later was back, saying he couldn't sleep. Small wonder, as he'd been doing little else all day. I took the opportunity to ask him what he remembered about August 5th (I was pretty far behind. August 5th was the first time we had been in Loliondo.) "Not much," he said, "except being in the back of Bagnall's truck with no mattress." I pointed out that he had had a mattress, two in fact, and he said he didn't see how I remembered such details. Nor did he remember, fortunately, that I had called him a sissy for taking two mattresses on what was supposed to be such a short trip. Changing the subject, he now complained about how cold he was. Maybe he did remember something because he then said he was "a sissy about the cold. But wait 'til we get to the Red Sea!" He often threatened us with the Red Sea when we complained of anything.

I realised that my passive attitude (I called it making the best of things) must have been extremely irritating to Pru. Somehow, the idea of continuing with Ansti had now became all my idea, as indeed had been the idea of going to Africa with him in the first place, while being sensible and getting a job in Nairobi became all hers. Besides, she knew that "my" Andrew was a lot nearer Loliondo than "her" Oliver, should either of them get our messages. What did she have to look forward to? Probably nothing but watching Andrew and me and more futile jungle-nighting. She was really getting tired of the whole thing.

When the District Officer happened to call by, we took the opportunity of asking Ansti if we could visit the on-going fair and cattle auction. This tactic combined surprise (no time for him to think of reasons why not) with making it awkward for him to refuse such a reasonable request in the D.O.'s presence. But Ansti was equal to any amount of strategy. He announced that he would take us himself. Then, the minute the D.O. had left, he decided we could go by ourselves, a much better outcome. But then he changed his mind again and said he didn't trust us with the power wagon. As by now he had revealed that Mr. Djillon was planning to take us back to Klein's Camp, he probably thought we'd try to get to the post office again, as indeed we would have. So he re-decided to take us. As we got in the truck, Pru then remarked that she was surprised he would go off leaving all his equipment lying around the rest house unguarded. I thought this a dangerous idea as Ansti would immediately say only one of us could go. He didn't, but a few minutes down the track to the auction grounds he stopped the truck and got out, saying he was worried about his stuff and walked back. Post Office, we thought at once. But we could hardly go back past Ansti, so we went on only to find no one at the "fair" such as it was (a few stalls) and no auction until the afternoon. We went back into Loliondo. The post office was closed. Brightly and innocently we turned up at the rest house hoping our supposed good behavior would result in getting the afternoon off. Twice during lunch Ansti remarked that he had heard heavy thunder and thought it was sure to rain. We read into this remark an incipient case of left-all-alone-again blues. We glowered at him. I suppose most of the time Ansti had no idea what he was being glowered at for. We had become so suspicious of his least statement that we read into it what wasn't there. In fact we were allowed to go to the cattle auction and even got a wave from Ansti as we drove away. This time the post office was open.

The auction was a very muddy affair. The Masai were there in thousands, the cattle for sale were herded by lots into a concrete walled enclosure on top of which, on one side, the buyers sat while the Masai owners hovered against the other, either hopping up and down or leaning stoically on their sticks, dressed in their best and elaborately coiffed, It was a pity there was no sun to show them off. David Reed, the buyer from Tanganyika Packers, sat on a stand built out over part of the paddock next to the D.O., then the auctioneer, an interpreter, the D.C. Narok and lastly one of the Masai chiefs. We two sat behind them with all the askaris. The planks seemed very wobbly with so many people on them.

Indian buyers, we were told, indicate the sum they want to bid by lifting their eyebrows, or even just one eyebrow. The auctioneer had to be very alert.

Outside the main enclosure were various makeshift corrals made of wooden slats into which cattle were being herded by the high-pitched calls of their owners. Beyond this dust and noise was yet another circle of, on one side, holding pens and on the other, at least six fires at which feasting was going on, with blood an guts strewn all over the ground. A sort of biltong was also being made from the leftovers. I think, but we didn't approach this area too closely. Every one of the Masai looked very wild; they were having the best time of their year. They were friendly to us, as always, especially when we produced the few Masai words we'd learned at Nondotto, and were very willing to be photographed. I let one of the *moran* look through my telephoto lens and he cackled shrilly then went around his companions, holding it up to each in turn and laughing at such a ridiculous sight.

We got back a bit late, but as it was drizzling, we didn't think Ansti would decide on a Jungle Night. We gave lifts to lots of jolly Masai, fourteen on the top and three to each running board and they enjoyed it hugely. We could hardly see to drive through the forest of legs hanging down from the roof of the cab. Ansti would not have approved and we hoped it would be too dark for him to see all that telltale red ochre. He didn't, but we were wrong about jungle-nighting. Ansti was busy with preparations. We commented that the mattress on top was soaked. But Ansti merely replied that if we had not had the truck all afternoon it wouldn't have been.

We set off, Pru driving. After a mile or so we slowed to a stop. Ansti rapped sharply on the cab roof. Pru's annoyed voice floated up: "the truck just won't go," she said. Ansti clambered down, a large wet patch on the seat of his pants. There was one on mine too, and it was cold now night had fallen. The trouble was simple enough. We had run out of fuel again, and this time it was clearly our fault. Ansti said he was "completely disillusioned" about us and accused us of gallivanting all over the place all afternoon, cross-questioning us about exactly how far the auction place was and so on. How much fuel there should have been occupied him for the rest of the evening. He said what a pity it was that he had slept all afternoon to prepare for a long jungle night. He said a lot of other things too. We didn't answer, just went to bed. We were due to leave for Klein's Camp with Mr. Djillon in the morning.

By eight we had cleaned up the rest house and packed, but Ansti, who had nothing to do but look after his own possessions was dissatisfied with everything and made us half an hour late at the duka, and at the duka confusion reigned. Our particular concern was returning the rest house key to the D.O., as one must, before leaving, and the *boma* was at the other end of town from the duka and the track to Klein's Camp. Ansti was very difficult about this and the supposed joy-riding of yesterday was thrown at us again. We also wanted to mail our letters home before leaving, but our mention of "post office" brought on another tirade. We could only imagine what Mr. Djillon thought.

After everything was stowed, Ansti loaded the shotgun and insisted on keeping it in the cab under our feet, but we didn't think it wise to argue. The whole morning seemed to have been spent arguing. We set off up the slippery track, following Mr. Djillon, Ansti driving. I could see he was angry about something , maybe everything. In a little while, he began to shake. He was holding onto the wheel but his upper body was going back and forth and his blue eyes staring, very wide open. He'd had a fit like this before somewhere so we knew something bad was coming and braced ourselves and out it came. He shouted at me that I and I alone was responsible for the death of Mrimi, the game scout. I had as good as killed him with my bare hands! I was joy-riding with the game ranger and made him go too fast. "I couldn't even keep up! If you hadn't been going so fast that fellow would never have fallen off!"

I said the game ranger was chasing poachers and how fast he went was nothing to do with me, but it seemed that Ansti had deeply resented the time spent catching poachers—his time, with his girls, as he saw it—and had obviously spent a month brooding about it. He added that he'd written as much to my mother. As the power wagon was now blundering all over the road, it was a bad time to argue with him but I was furious. "You can't mean anything so stupid," I said. "How can you even think like that?" But it was no use.

When we came to the first river crossing, Ansti got out leaving the door open and in getting back in he kicked the gun and it went off. This felt like the last straw. We made a pact not to speak to him. Maybe he was trying to force us to resign so he could say we had broken our contract? Maybe today's tirade was only the first instalment? Maybe Pru was right and the whole thing was hopeless.

We Get Fired

The worst part of this second trip to Klein's Camp, aside from Ansti's accusations, was the presence of Mr. Djillon, our Indian white hunter. Mr. Djillon had been perfectly nice in his shop, but in the bush he took command and behaved as the lord of the jungle, and of us. We ate at his table and of his food which consisted of a vegetable curry swimming in ghee for every meal, prepared indifferently by his Masai cook. This alone was depressing, but he took to ordering us about and during the day he placed the charpoy he rested on in full view of the access to our tent. We couldn't seem to get out of his sight. Ansti also behaved strangely in Djillon's presence. The accent business was now very pronounced, and his table manners, never good, became worse. The only blessing was that we were apparently not now required for jungle night expeditions. Ansti and Mr. Djillon went off by themselves. Mr. Djillon had shot an antelope on the way to the camp; they had hung it up right away and then every night went back to their kill. Like dogs or wild beasts in the bush, we thought savagely.

Pru and I became desperate to get out of the camp, and one day had a minor showdown, about washing our hair. In spite of the recent rain, the Klein's camp water supply was still indifferent and we announced that we wanted to go to the Bolongonya. We said we would walk there, but Mr. Djillon wouldn't hear of that and insisted on taking us. We protested but eventually gave in, saying we would walk back. Ansti now announced that he too would come to the Bolongonya. Could we never get away from them? A constant worry was that Andrew or Oliver, but probably Andrew, might turn up. Would they or he have enough sense to keep out of sight? What if one of them were even now camped at the Bolongonya? There would be a most unpleasant scene.

To our relief the place was empty and after further argument we finally persuaded the two men not to watch us washing ourselves (and our hair) but actually to *Go Away*. Freedom! It went to our heads. We splashed and washed and laughed with relief. At about noon, we started back, soon losing all the benefit of our bathe but still euphoric. We never gave lions or rhinos a thought. It was all open country with only the odd herd of dusty tommy or kongoni grazing peacefully and showing no sign of alarm. Open country in Africa seemed far too large for two girls and any dangerous beast to meet up and we completed the six miles uneventfully. Back at Klein's camp we found to our joy we had missed the curry and so had a lunch of our own choosing, and two beers because we were so thirsty, which left us feeling a bit heady in the middle of the day. It started to drizzle, then rain in earnest so we went to our tent for a nap, waking to find a river of mud running over the ground sheet. We hoped Ansti's and Mr. Djillon's beds had been left out, but no such luck.

By night time, the weather had cleared and Ansti decided that we would all go jungle-nighting, and that this time he would be "net boy" and I (to my surprise) was told to do the photography while Mr. Djillon managed the light. There were no protests. We found a lion at the kill tearing happily at the gazelle's stomach and I quite enjoyed taking pictures of Ansti trying to creep up on him to throw the net, which he did, scuttling quickly back to the safety of the truck. The lion merely growled and went on eating. As Mr. Djillon still had the light on I went on taking pictures until Ansti told us both to stop, and we noticed with satisfaction that Ansti did not seem anxious (as net boy) to retrieve the net which was lying a foot or so from the lion's tail. Instead he got up on top with Mr. Djillon and we sat in the cab. We all stared to the unappetizing scene for a while until Ansti clambered down and appeared outside the cab window. "Djillon," he complained loudly, "is drunk! Snoring up there on my time!" We were secretly delighted. Ansti ordered a return to camp and then as a punishment he took Mr. Djillon back to the kill, where they both spent the night.

The next morning we decided to go for another "walk." Yesterday's jaunt had gone very well. This time we prepared to spend the day away. Under the guise of taking camera equipment, we packed two Tusker beers and some chocolate into a bag with our books, paints and fly swats. We intended to lie up by some stream, perhaps the Grumetti further down. We didn't want to excite Ansti's suspicions by heading in the direction of Banagi, but when out of sight we intended to do just this in the hope that if Andrew was on his way to us we could intercept him. We sauntered slowly out of camp. No one said bossily that we ought to have a game scout with us. I don't know what made us think Andrew Bagnall would turn up. Hadn't he told us that he was off to the Mara River in the opposite direction? Nevertheless, our many calculations of the probable speed of the telegraph system and when he might pass through Musoma (where he would pick up the message) all encouraged us to think we might be "rescued" soon. Maybe even today? There was that game department order to keep an eye on us, after all.

We started walking more briskly, the beer clinking away. Were we far enough out of camp? We stopped. Even over the noise of the bottles we had heard something—an engine—a land rover? Yes. We couldn't see who was driving with the sun on the windscreen, but it was Andrew all right, with Banana in the truck not far behind. We poured out a rather confused tale over the door, then, displacing Muchoto, got in and were driven to yet another camp site just across the Grumetti from Klein's Camp proper. This seemed rather close to us, but we all sat down under a tree and with the aid of beer and chocolate filled Andrew in with the details. We kept looking around, nervously. Once I thought I saw one of Mr. Djillon's boys dodge behind the trees. We were very apprehensive and Andrew laughed at us. But suddenly there was the familiar roar of the power wagon which nosed over the hill about six feet from where we were sitting. No time to do anything. The door burst open and Ansti leapt out, arm and fist extended and ran straight at Andrew who received the fist near his eye before he could get up from the ground. Andrew rocked backward, saying "See here, Carapace!" But Ansti was coming at him again, so Andrew, now on his feet, hit him on the upper lip. Andrew's nose was bleeding, but Ansti's lip bled more. We were shouting at them to stop. The various boys stood around us with blank faces. I leapt on Ansti's back, but he didn't feel me. Pru tried to hold Andrew. Futile. Finally I got between them. I suppose we should have stayed out of it, but by now we were as mad as they were. Over my head, Ansti was shouting at Andrew about how we had killed Mrimi and how he was going to report it, and how if any game ranger came near his camp again to steal his girls he would have him run in, and he was going to fire these damned girls the minute he got them back to Nairobi. "Fire us now," said Pru. "Fire us right now, here in the bush. We don't care! But you're too cheap to fire us!"

"All right," said Ansti. "I fire you." He climbed into the power wagon and drove off.

We all sat down again, Andrew's nose bleed had stopped, but there was caked blood all over his moustache. He brushed our solicitude aside. We had some more beer. Pru and I decided we'd have to brave Ansti to collect our belongings. And after that? Andrew said he would take us back to Banagi, but not for a couple of days, because he was actually here looking for animals for some "wretched safari" that had been dumped on him—he had not received our telegram. We could think about what we were going to do once we were in Banagi.

Banana drove us to the door of our tent. Ansti was sitting not far away, his head in his hands, the picture of misery. We ignored him. We thought he was miserable at having to pay an extra airfare home.

Observed closely by Mr. Djillon who stood in the door flap of our tent, we rolled up our bed rolls—well, Ansti's bed rolls technically but we could settle that later. We had to have them for now—and packed our stuff. Mr. Djillon kept trying to persuade us not to leave poor Mr. Carapace who was so unhappy. Our expressions were stony. We just wished he'd stay out of it. We told him that anything to discuss we'd discuss directly with Mr. Carapace, thank you. Mr. Djillon countered that Mr. Carapace was crying. We asked him to move aside so we could put or things in the land rover. He stood his ground. "You will not leave Mr. Carapace," he insisted. "He is too sad." We brushed by him, got into the land rover and were driven off.

At Andrew's camp we had some lunch. Muchoto made us feel right at home by at once announcing *"Nyama hakuna, Bwana,"* (no meat) but Andrew just shrugged. I couldn't tell what he was thinking, but he did not look very pleased to see me again. Pru thought we should ask him to send us back to Banagi at once, where we might get a lift to Musoma with the Bramble. I was, naturally, less keen on this idea but had no chance to ask Andrew his opinion. The minute he'd eaten, he pushed off with the game scouts to find the elusive game. From his expression, such as it was, I decided he thought we were just another burden, like the other wretched safari, when what he really wanted was to be left alone.

We went down to the stream to wash. While we were there, Andrew's boys kept popping out of the bushes to offer their sympathy. *"Mze kali,* Memsahib, *mbaya sana…"* ("Fierce old man, very bad.") We were pleased, but found it difficult to wash more than our hands. There seemed to be a lot of boys around even though Andrew was operating on a reduced safari staff, having had to leave people behind in Banagi to look after "the Dar-es-Salaam fellow." This made us feel even more of a burden.

After supper, Andrew was just getting out a cheroot for a quiet smoke when Mr. Djillon turned up. He said Mr. Carapace didn't consider he had really fired us and was about to elaborate when Andrew brushed aside further words and asked to see his license. It transpired that he didn't have one and Andrew told him firmly that he was going to "run him in."

There were no sounds of jungle night that night. All was quiet, just the murmur of boys laughing in the background. Was Ansti sobbing in his tent?

"A short life of trouble, dear girl(s)
Old man with a broken heart"

Then Pru started. "I thought I heard a shot!" This was unlikely but for a while we wondered. Still, in Africa, nothing stays hidden for long. No one came running, so we all went to bed, Pru and I on the ground in Andrew's tent, and Andrew on his camp bed under a fly sheet rigged up by his boys among the trees.

The next morning Andrew took us with him to explore more of northern Tanganyika, an area of increasingly beautiful country — lovely shady upper reaches of the Bolongonya and more of the rolling golden hills west of Loliondo, so different from the Serengeti's vast plains. We ended up in a sort of gorge filled with wild fig trees whose twisted roots were embedded in a thick carpet of leaves. I think most of the figs were probably dying from the drought, such was the difference in rainfall between the Loliondo area and where we were, but shade from their branches fell lacily on

In the shade of the fig trees

the ground, providing us with as much shelter from the sun as we could ask for. We drank beer at intervals, but had no lunch. There were plenty of flies, but there are always plenty of flies. On the way back to camp, Andrew shot a tommy, and we decided to have shish-kebab and rice with cabbage and nuts for supper. We cooked the meat ourselves on unreliable skewers of wood, the hand holding the skewer wrapped in cloth and one arm across the face as protection from the fierce heat of the flames. It was delicious.

We heard no more from Ansti.

We went into thicker bush the next day, with thicker swarms of flies. We saw a giant hornbill, but none of the big game Andrew was looking for. It was breathlessly hot, too hot to do anything. It was my mother's birthday in nine days, but there was no prospect of posting a letter, and some reluctance even to start all the explanations. Andrew said he was going to the Bolongonya and Pru hitched a lift, to wash her hair again. I opted to disappear into a book. They were soon back, Pru giggling. She said Andrew had given her a bare ten minutes for all operations before he returned, tooting his horn.

In another day or so we left for Banagi. On the way we tried to buy Andrew a case of beer at the duka in Ikoma, but he wouldn't let us. He said if we wanted to help, we could paint the inside of his house instead: he was trying "to spruce the place up a bit." We found the "Dar-es-Salaam fellow" and his party absent, which was nice, and we had a good meal, cooked by Saidi. Andrew said a few days of Muchoto's cooking would make anything taste good and Muchoto went off in a huff.

The very next day, Oliver turned up, out of the blue, followed by Alan. This caused a big celebration. The Bramble also called in, back from Musoma with the paint. His first question was "What have you done with Carapace?"

We could now get on with the decorating and started with the *choo*. I mixed a large quantity of blue distemper and slapped it on the inside walls. The next day, we mixed some "terracotta" from the earth and copied onto the blue surface some of the cave paintings reproduced in the latest Tanganyika archaeological journal. Terracotta on blue looked very fine, and depending on which way you faced when seated at your business, you could contemplate Alan's very fierce buffalo, or Andrew's magnificent hunt involving wildebeest and every kind of antelope with plenty of arrows flying around, or my abduction of a village maiden by a party of warriors whose maleness was not in dispute. We were all very pleased with the results, and I discovered years later that the paintings lasted long after there were no more game rangers at Banagi, but that's another story. The rooms of the house were much less interesting to do: no art work. It was after all a government building. In the midst of all this, the D.C. Musoma arrived unannounced, with his wife and three small children, to spend a couple of days in the Serengeti looking at lions.

When they had left, Andrew, without a word of explanation, pushed off on another safari into the bush. I only found out later that this "separation" had been self-imposed, to allow me to "make up my mind." I had pretty well done so already, even with so many people around, but we had hardly had time for private chats. Oliver left too. We had at least managed to settle the details of the proposed elephant hunt. Oliver said he'd meet us under a certain conspicuous baobab south of Mwanza, near Sangameatu, on October 15th unless he heard to the contrary. Alan, who had been rather left out so far, now had both of us on his hands. He was very charming, but his chosen topics of conversation were always a joke between Pru and me: the disposal of his parents' ashes, a rotting corpse he'd seen on a road, or the child with impetigo, as well as the inevitable tommy dissections. He also mentioned a girl scientist in England, speaking of her very fondly. Good, we thought, he does have a girl somewhere. We were busy with our private dreams.

The man from Dar-es-Salaam came back the next day. He said he was in public relations, and appeared to be alone. When he found out who we were, he said that the Carapace safari "stinks throughout the Territory" (Tanganyika Territory) and that we, Pru and I, were now regarded as "two unfortunate girls, well out of a fate worse than death, rescued by a kindly game ranger." So far so good. "But where is the game ranger?" he asked, and we all said we didn't know. "When will he be back?" We didn't know that either. "Rum," he said. "Rescues two girls then does a bunk? Queer chap, I must say. He was supposed to take me out, too."

Fortunately Andrew returned that night, took the public relations man "out" the next day, spent the whole of the next in his office and then announced he had to go to Musoma for his Swahili exam. Passing the language exam was an essential step in gaining promotion and a salary hike. I decided to go with him to deal with a septic thumb. I had not yet been able to extract a long, stiff piece of grass, driven into it the day Mrimi died, and by now it was swollen and painful.

In Musoma I picked up news of Ansti. He'd passed through town the week before, looking worried and asking everyone where we were. People thought he looked quite pathetic. "What have you girls been doing to him? He had us crying in our beers." One man said that he believed Andrew probably had been misleading Carapace about good places to find game, "to make the safari last longer," he suggested, winking at me. "Certainly not," I said hotly. "That's one of Ansti's stories. He thinks up all sorts of lies." The man shrugged.

Andrew had told our friend the manageress that he wanted dinner early, and had told me to be ready on time. But now where was he? I was waiting for him in the bar, and being pinned down by yet another Peter, and Pearl had been in at least twice to say our food was ready. Finally she sent this Peter off to look for Andrew. Sensibly, Peter went to Andrew's room (as I had) but Peter, getting no answer, threw open the door. And there he was, fast asleep. This was the third time he'd been found sound asleep when he was supposed to be elsewhere. What was the matter with him? Did he have narcolepsy? He explained that when he found all the bathrooms occupied, he had "just lain down for a minute."

The doctor who examined my thumb prescribed three days of penicillin injections so I was dumped unceremoniously on the District .Commissioner. and his wife while Andrew went back to Banagi. They didn't seem to mind even though they were about to go on safari to the Mara, all of them. Watching them from the sidelines, helping when I could, I thought the tempers of the three children and everyone else were much strained by this exercise and that if I had been the D.C. I would have gone by myself. The day of departure was especially fraught. The ferry service from Musoma to North Mara depended, as everyone in the Territory well knew, more on the state of the captain's liver than on natural phenomena like wind and wave. Because of the uncertainty no one, not even the children, had any breakfast. I also had to run to the hospital to collect my vials of penicillin, so that I might have the stuff administered by various "dressers" on the way.

On the last day of this trip, in some out station, we attended the christening of the District Officer's latest child. It was very hot, and the baby extremely angry. The ceremony was attended by the local judge, two doctors, the two richest Indian shop keepers, an anthropologist working in the area, some police and agricultural officers, two chaps from Shell and of course the Bishop, accompanied by his shadow, Ted, the parson. Ted was a small man, mostly nose, kindly and shy, but he made me very nervous by keeping his eyes fixed somewhere about the level of my hips while we were talking. Towards the end of the evening, he sat with his arm around the Bishop. The anthropologist, from the London School of Economics, suggested I whip up a phonemic analysis of Ki-Ikoma while I was at Banagi. I suspected one-upmanship.

We also met the new D.C.'s new wife, young, nervous, fresh out from England. (my host was soon going on leave and the new D.C. would take his place.). There was also a woman who said she could never get her jellies to set, and of course the D.O.'s other children. The new D.C. also had a child, by a previous wife, a boy with exactly the same curious shape of head as his father. Probably all his children, no matter the mother, will have that head. Once genes like that get loose, Nature shows no mercy.

The time before Andrew was to collect me passed very slowly, and even once we were at last back in Musoma another day was added by a message from him to say he had lots of *shauris* to settle. When he did come, he put a bloody Grant's gazelle leg on the hall table in payment for the D.C.'s hospitality. I felt like a chattel. Furthermore, everyone at the christening had kept telling me what a "good, steady chap" Andrew was. Instead of being pleased I felt, once again, "settled." As we left, the D.C.'s wife announced her intention of coming back to Banagi "soon" with not only her children but the judge, his wife and his child as well. Andrew paled slightly, but was cordial. I suppose all these kind people thought the life in Banagi must be unbearably lonely.

At the hotel, Pearl put her arms around both of us. "I especially didn't tell your Mr. Carapace *anything*," she said, and winked, "though I just knew where you'd be!" She poked me in the ribs. "Just look at them—the dears!" she carolled to all and sundry.

Halfway back to Banagi, with only a few Africans in the land rover with us, felt relatively peaceful and we decided to stop and have a beer under a tree. But Andrew was immediately pounced on by a scout who turned up to apply for leave (we were near his village). There was a long discussion about the number of people due to arrive at Banagi and what they were to be shown; it was decided he could not be spared. We reached Banagi at about nine to find Pru reading by herself in the living room and very hungry, having put off dinner for our benefit.

To our alarm, Mrs. D.C.'s "soon" apparently meant the next day! We were all up really early the next morning. While I'd been away, Andrew had let the local *fundi* loose in the only big bedroom and it was a shambles. We cleared him out, protesting, and set up a sort of dormitory for the women and children. Pru and I retained our small sanctuary while Alan was moved in with Andrew. I thought the Judge could bunk in with them too, but Alan said three was too many so he was put on the verandah. Saidi announced as usual that there was no meat, so Andrew went off and shot some antelopes.

All of them arrived at tea time and were sent out again as soon as possible to look at lions. They were soon back, flushed with pleasure and saying how lucky we were to be living in the midst of all this obliging game. Between drinks and dinner the house was reduced to chaos. All the children had to be bathed and then all the adults (except us — there wasn't enough water), then the children had to be fed, and then the adults. Saidi looked on with his eyes popping. I hoped he was not blaming all this frantic domesticity on me. Even Andrew, who managed to ignore most inconveniences, was irritable.

On the other hand, after everyone had gone to bed somewhere, we were briefly alone. In such moments we'd plan what our life was going to be like at Banagi and looked forward to the rains which kept guests away.

More lion-watching was scheduled for the next day. There was a long discussion among our guests about whether of not they'd be back for lunch. The judge, a man who cared for his comforts, voted to return, but Mrs. D.C. said what fun it would be to have it out. They had it out. Peace! I was able to finish the wall painting. We were due to leave ourselves the next day.

The Elephant Hunt

The ivory of one elephant a year, taken on licence, made an important financial contribution to a game ranger's low salary, and the timing and general location of this year's hunt had been planned a long time. Pru and I, now included, thought we'd probably go directly back to Nairobi from southern Tanganyika and wanted to take our stuff with us, but Andrew said that as he was taking Saidi and three game scouts and only the short wheel base land rover with a small trailer, we had to leave non-essentials in Banagi. As it was, with two tents and six people, food and beer, we were heavily loaded. We also picked up Charles, he of the papayas, on the way. It was a 200 mile trip to Mwanza, the last two thirds through Sukumuland, dry and desolate. Andrew said he hated this part of Tanganyika where there was little game and every other headman was a witch. "Wizard, actually," I said and he favored me with a look. We managed the journey without breakdowns, however, only delayed at one ferry crossing by a grossly overloaded lorry which had fallen into the river between the ferry and dry land on the far side. After waiting an hour under a tree, Andrew had himself poled across in a canoe, whose owner was doing brisk opportune business, and told the ferry master to _____ and the lorry was unloaded and shoved out of the way.

I shall always think of Mwanza as rocks and heat. Even Lake Victoria looked hot, a blazing blue too bright to keep one's eyes on. We weren't given long in this outpost at the lake's southern end, but were driven fast down the dusty main street and on to the house of Andrew's friends, the Tanners, where we would be spending the night. Penny, thin and pretty, with large pale eyes, made us at home immediately, while Ralph pounced on Andrew to tell him all about his work among the Wa-Sukumu, interrupted with difficulty only when tea was served. Tea was lavish. There were not only the usual slices of bread with butter and lemon curd and three other types of jam but also a large heavy cake, thickly iced with Andrew's initials on it in pink for his recent birthday. It was quite overwhelming in all that heat. Ralph said, "Penny has been slaving for days;" she looked embarrassed, telling him not to be so silly, whereupon he resumed his energetic talking to Andrew until we rose to bathe and change for dinner. During the evening while Ralph was still going strong, Penny found out from us that after the elephant hunt, Pru and I were planning to look for jobs in Nairobi. "Ralph," she cried, "listen to this!" She explained, and at once Ralph abandoned Andrew and took charge of our futures. Penny was to take Pru to see a Mrs. Hotchkiss, whoever she was, and I was to be taken to the headquarters of the filariasis society when we again passed through Mwanza after the hunt. Ralph claimed that "these poor people" had had a vacancy for an anthropologist "for ages." I thought it unlikely they would want a girl of 21 with a mere BA. I also had no desire to get into something I couldn't get out of. "Alternatively," Ralph said, "you could do up my Sukumu dictionary and live in in return." I thought Penny looked a little unhappy at this, and Andrew gave me a warning glance. After this we were soon organised into bed with the words, "Shall we let the girls lead off?" There was no chance for even a word with Andrew. He was locked out of the house to sleep in his tent in the yard.

We escaped the next morning to get some last minute things in Mwanza, and Andrew told me that Ralph had told him he and Penny were seriously worried about Pru "associating with" a man like Oliver Fenton. "For heaven's sake, why?" I asked. He says, said Andrew, Oliver already has a wife somewhere, and that he was involved in quite unsavoury rackets in Burma during the war, and that he had chopped two men up with an axe, beheading them, among other things. It all sounded fantastic, preposterous even, but people often believe the wildest gossip. I wondered gloomily if all this was even now being recounted to Pru. She had been in a bad mood for days. Only that morning she had told me that she now thought she did not really care for Oliver and was "going through with" the elephant hunt only for my sake. This gossip will really put the lid on things, I thought, and indeed when we got back I found that Penny had told every word of all this to Pru, who was crying in our room.

It was therefore with some embarrassment that we found the Tanners ready and waiting to celebrate Andrew's and my "engagement" with a bottle of champagne and more cake. We had said nothing about being engaged, yet everywhere we went we were being slotted into place as a couple, while Pru, having just decided against marrying Oliver, and who now believed she had been deceived by him, was faced with his company for the next two weeks. "Man," as Mr. Djillon would have said, there would be trouble ahead.

No time for it now, though. Ralph had organized our afternoon: rock-climbing. Penny was able to refuse, lucky her. Andrew and Ralph were practising for their assault on the mountain, Oldonyo Lengai, later in the month.. We all duly struggled up a rock chimney and at the top were allowed a brief respite to look out over the lake. At this height, we could see all the islands, lush with dark green foliage, dotting the blue water of the bay. Beautiful. Andrew took lots of pictures, not of the bay but of us, sweaty and dishevelled. I knew he was mailing such things back to his parents and begged him to stop. Ralph commented that "shiny noses come out better," and we rolled our eyes. I can't believe now that we cared about how shiny our noses were, but we did—in 1953, in photos to be sent to our, and his, no doubt nicely powdered mothers.

That evening, we went out to a neighbor's for dinner and met there the French wife of the local sociologist. She seemed very starchy and was dressed in a curious yellow garment of great complexity. I thought that I was perhaps supposed to converse with her husband on professional terms but all I could think of was the story Andrew had told me about her. Some months ago, Eric Wilson, the new D.C. whom I had met in the Mara with his new wife, had visited Mwanza. Andrew said that Eric was one of the very few soldiers ever to receive a posthumous V.C. in the war and subsequently to have come to life. On his visit, Madame Sociologist had taken him aside and said, in her attractive accent, "Tell me, Colonel Wilson, how did you get your V.D.?

We sent a lot of telegrams before we left Mwanza, to friends of friends we planned to visit in Kenya and to our parents with vague assurances, then headed for the bush, picking up yet another game scout. It was still relentlessly hot and dry and we rode with our feet on the bar over the dashboard to get them away from the engine. We found Oliver, as planned, sitting under the conspicuous baobab. He had been there for a day, his pup tent barely visible beyond his battered land rover. His first words, besides greeting Pru who mumbled something, were: "So sorry, people, but I didn't bring any beer" (Andrew's face fell) "and the vegetables are all spoiled." Oliver was not popular that night. We camped in an empty schoolhouse without water or beer. Andrew read his mail, silently. Oliver had no news of Ansti. Well, that was something, but we did not suppose Ansti was sitting quietly anywhere, enjoying life. He was probably up to something. We were still nervous of home reactions. I thought of writing the postponed letter to my mother about Andrew and me and the future, but it was too hot.

Up at sunrise, we set off across the flat country. We were heading for the nearest duka as a start: sugar for the boys, beer if possible for us. We were heading southeast over land so dry and dusty and so almost featureless that small native encampments appeared shallowly and suddenly as slight swellings of the ground; sometimes there were a few clumps of rocks. Not a blade of grass, What did the cattle live on? We must have crossed twenty or thirty river beds, all dry. The duka, when we reached it, had no beer. We made some tea instead and went on to our first camp. No camp as such, with a name, just a place Oliver knew of near another dry river bed where elephants might come to dig for water with their tusks. To hunt in the dry season, and near the end of it at that, ensures that the elephants will be found near whatever water, or smell of water, remains.

When we stopped, one of the scouts said he thought he heard the sound of elephants feeding, breaking off leafy branches with their trunks, and we soon found them and watched them for a while. No worthwhile ivory among them; Andrew decided to get some good photos instead and covered by Oliver with a heavy gun (a .475) he crept close, retreating hastily when the herd started to move.

Andrew photographing elephants

In the afternoon, at the hottest time of the day, we explored a nearby riverbed deeply cut, for that part of the country, into the surrounding land. Its steep sides were promisingly eroded in many places by the tread of heavy feet and some surface water still lay in shallow pools, ankle deep and deliciously cool. We returned to the camp to find Andrew's lean-to shelter had been set up by the boys as bath headquarters and we washed more or less in the open, welcoming the breeze on our bareness, a change from our chilly sufferings of two months ago.

In the morning we were up early before the sun, Andrew already eager to be off. We had agreed that two searching parties moving through the bush were better than one, though I wondered how Pru with her burden of secret thoughts would fare as she followed Oliver. If her day was anything like mine with Andrew, she had no time to brood on anything besides flies, heat and thorns. Andrew stretched out his long legs and strode ahead, leaving a strung out line of game scouts behind him, with me, feeling faint for lack of breakfast and rather vulnerable, bringing up the rear. After an hour and a half, we visited a small village to ask for news of elephants - "*habari ya tembo?*" While Andrew was talking, I gratefully accepted an invitation to enter the chief's hut. The doorway was very low, its sides smoothed by the placing of many hands to help their owners through, and I thought the inside of the roof must also have a glassy surface from the bumping of many heads but it was too dark to see. I sat on the proffered stool to nurse my worst blister. There were no decorations on the walls and only a few crude implements were lying around, among them an old can opener, very rusty. Unfortunately the chief had no news of elephant, so we left the village and walked for another two hours seeing nothing but thorn bush. By now even the birds had stopped flying around. I finally unloaded my six pounds of cine camera onto a game guard and caught up with Andrew to suggest a rest break. He seemed to ignore every rare bit of shade in spite of my hovering at his heels but eventually turned around to ask vaguely if I would like some breakfast "fairly soon." It was only when I said I could not go a step further without something, even though I knew the something would be no more than a few nuts and raisins, that he did at last stop. After this we walked and walked and I did not ask to stop again, having reached the stage of not daring to stop for fear of collapse, and at last we were rewarded by seeing one elephant, then two, then a whole herd of them slowly moving past us. We had completed a sort of circle by this time and another hour brought us within sight of our camp where there was actually food waiting on a table, marked by a telltale cloud of flies.

In the evening, we had a "clearing of the air," the process much favored by Pru. I was only surprised it had not happened before. Oliver told his side of the Tanners' stories two or three times, denying the wife and pleading extreme provocation for the killings, and it all sounded believable; he was such a likeable fellow one did not willingly believe ill of him. Nor was he much offended by the rumors. Besides, he and Pru had seen far more elephant than we had, which put both elephant hunters in a good mood, a prelude to a pleasant evening. Andrew experimented with a "Banagi cocktail," and we all got a little tight.

The next day I got the curse, so called, but this time I regarded it as a blessing. With a clear conscience, I elected to stay in camp, alone except for six people, while Andrew went out alone trailed by his scouts. I was sure he would not miss me. Our elephant hunting could scarcely be called companionable. To my surprise, this day everyone came back early. The elephants were said to be quite close by, and approaching them from higher ground we found them browsing among some trees. All of us—Oliver, Pru, me, the game scouts—clambered onto a convenient pile of rocks while Andrew, covered by Oliver, crept closer for a good photograph. In the opinion of the stay-behinds, he got rather too close. We saw an elderly female separate herself from the herd and stand facing him, her ears spread and swaying her trunk. Oliver called to Andrew. Andrew got up and then paused, stooped for something, then ran from her trumpeting charge. Now everything happened at once. Andrew leapt onto the rocks, Oliver's gun went off over my head, then Andrew's; the elephant still seemed to be coming at us, filling my view finder with her head. Just as suddenly she collapsed and died at the foot of our rock pile. "Why did you stop?" I asked Andrew. "Oh I wanted to pick up my spare lens," he said, which made Oliver mad. "Too bad we had to shoot her. No ivory either." The elephant was very old, her tusks cracked and yellow. The carcass was given to the local chief and in a few hours the delighted tribesmen were inside her belly searching for treasured organs. while others sawed at her feet, preparatory to making a tasty soup. One man posed grinning for Pru and her camera with the elephant's vagina dripping blood from his hands. Vultures waited, circling overhead.

The dead elephant

We moved on the next day to a place we called the Palm Tree River Camp. Though not on any map as such, it was a distinctive-looking place. The river bed was seasonal, a wide swathe of sand flowing between banks of borassus palms. The strong contrasts between the glare of the sand, the almost black borassus leaves and bright orange fruit made an effective picture, but I buried several efforts in the sand before I produced anything worth keeping. I then got out a small lump of plasticine I had with me and amused myself by trying to sculpt Andrew's head. Soon all the men wanted their heads done, and I had to make one head out of another which might have upset a more superstitious lot. We were camped some distance from the river among a grove of fig trees which provided pleasant shade but even so we soon tired of the heat and the swarms of flies and decided to explore further up the river where the scouts had found some elephant spoor. Until now we had been following what to me were mostly invisible signs of the passing of elephants; here, the sand was crisscrossed with the large round depressions left by their feet, and some smaller ones too, and their dung was everywhere. We followed one particular set of prints for a while, ankle deep in the burning sand, but gave up when we came to a track to a village. Andrew wanted to talk to the headman.

I had not yet seen such a picturesque village in East Africa. The huts were round and covered with hides like those of the Masai, but they were not surrounded by thorn brush kraals since there were fewer animals to protect. As a result the village seemed spacious, and the mature palms gave some shade, an asset the Masai do not bother about. We were at once offered an opened borassus nut to eat; it tasted sticky and sweet like overripe mango. The entire village smelled of these nuts, evidently in various stages of fermentation. The people were most hospitable and I was invited into every hut we passed; by the evidence most of them housing goats as well as people. On the way back to our own camp, I took a path of my own choosing and came across some men carrying salt who had come all the way from Lake Eyasi. I asked for "news" but all they said was "Dry, very dry." Nor had the headman any recent news of elephant. Judging by the bored expressions of those listening, he was only retelling the exploits of former years.

The heat was more intense than ever the next day. Oliver and Pru went off after breakfast; Andrew had left early without breakfast, and I stayed in camp. When Oliver and Pru came back, I took myself off to the sand river to do more sketching. Except for the riverine vegetation, everything had been recently burned; the blackened waist high stems and branches and the soot on the soil seemed to augment the heat. My sketches did not come out well. I got back to the camp to find that Andrew had returned and was in a foul mood. Though he generally went much further than Oliver, Oliver seemed to see more elephant, but neither had yet seen a worthwhile tusker. We were out of drink too.

The next day we moved to the promised "beautiful fort on top of towering cliffs:" Mkalama, an outpost of the former German East Africa. It did not quite live up to this description, and Andrew was much teased; still, it was on relatively higher ground, the roof was still intact and the rooms paved with stone, a welcome relief from hot sand. We could only spend one night there as the D.C. was expected. That night under a sky bright with stars, we strolled the castellated ramparts. It was quite romantic; as our paths crossed and re-crossed I wondered if Pru was falling in love with Oliver again. We didn't spend much time talking to each other these days. Long after the others had gone to bed, I sat alone on a wall. There was a very slight breeze It was perfectly quiet. In the moonlight, out on the surrounding plain, each acacia was silhouetted against the ground.

Oliver and Pru took off early the next morning for a particular camp Andrew had in mind, located at the foot of the rift wall near Lake Eyasi. A cleft in the wall at this point was said to have permanent water with palms and pools, all invisible until one was actually there. Oliver managed to follow Andrew's rather vague directions better than Andrew himself (the area was in Oliver's territory) but he picked a different camp site to the one Andrew had in mind. Andrew, who had without thinking about it been assuming that he was in charge of the expedition, its staff (his) and the tents (his) now found that Oliver refused to move his camp, consisting of his land rover and lean-to shelter. Nor would Andrew adopt Oliver's site. Oliver also claimed that Andrew's choice of water supply was fifty percent baboon urine. Andrew challenged him to find a better one. Andrew then enquired if his boys, who up to now had been doing the cooking for everyone, were no longer to do so, in which case would Oliver be joining us for "dinner" or not? This did not go down at all well. Oliver announced that he and Pru would both be "out" and stalked off. I laughed but no one else did. When we got around to bathing, I noticed that the water indeed smelled strongly but it seemed wise not to remark on it. The tent for Pru and me was set up halfway between the two camps, also the table and chairs; Oliver had none of these luxuries and the next night, when the invitation to dine was formally returned, we ate on the ground.

By now Oliver had decided the whole hunt was a waste of time and said he would "push off" back to Mto wa Mbu along the shores of Lake Eyasi. Pru and I had arranged to visit friends in Kenya on November 2nd but this was still a week away. "If you would care to join me," Andrew offered, "we could all go to Shinyanga to visit the diamond mines." He had meant to go for some time, he said, as the mine owner wanted to make a game reserve there. I waited to see what Pru would say. She shrugged and consented. She hadn't much choice. Besides, Shinyanga had a "hotel," and water.

The mines Andrew meant were very dusty and dry and filled with old, rusty machinery, and lay next door to Williamson's, a much grander establishment surrounded by a very high and modern electric fence. The proprietor of the mines we were visiting said Williamson's were very mean, and made "difficulties." His wife, dressed in black with a white lace collar, showed us a few diamonds in a drawer and then we were taken outside, given a clod of earth each with a "million to one" chance of finding a diamond in it and left to wander around while Andrew and the proprietor discussed their business. Andrew's two boys lay in his land rover, sleeping soundly. Not for the first time, we envied them their ability to do this anytime, anywhere.

We reached Mwanza the next afternoon in time for tea, which we had first at a hotel and then again at the Tanners. Pru was not at all keen to see the Tanners again with all the obvious explanations this would involve, but our return visit had been "arranged" and so we duly turned up, though two days early due to the aborting of the elephant hunt. Gamely they made us welcome. To Pru's and my consternation, they also had a slew of mail for us: letters from home demanding to know what on earth we were doing, one from the American Consul in Nairobi who had been bullied by Ansti into asking the same question, and a telegram from Ansti saying he had reported us missing to the Police. Hearing this, Andrew sent us both down at once to the Mwanza Police Station in his land rover, where we were treated quite severely by the Indian Police Commissioner, who neither accepted nor understood any of our explanations. We began to wonder if Ansti would succeed in having us ignominiously deported. It took a visit from Andrew to the police the next morning, on our way back to Banagi, to smooth things over.

At the Barata "Savoy" the proprietor had somehow got the news that Andrew and I were to be married and insisted on giving us two of the white hens innocently pecking at crumbs around our feet. They were at once trussed up and thrust under the seats to arrive in Banagi covered in mud, cold, weary like the rest of us: we had run into heavy rain and got stuck several times. As usual we stopped at the duka in Ikoma for supplies and the hospitable Mr.Metz, the owner, insisted we stay for food. "The Kuenzlers are already here," he said. He ushered us into a room full of beds in the center of which a table was piled with all the accompaniments for curry. His quiet, shy wife brought in two more plates, and Mr. Metz did the honors, saying "yes, please" with each small dish he passed. In one dish were some innocent-looking small red things and though I tried to treat everything with caution I must somehow have swallowed a whole one and had to retire weeping to the edge of one of the beds. Everyone laughed heartily except Mr. Metz, who was far too polite and stood beside me passing me tissues and saying yes please with each one.

In the "White Highlands"

Back at Banagi we thought the boys did not look in the least pleased to see us, certainly not Muchoto. They must have been hoping for a return to normality and a trouble-free bachelor establishment and here we were again. At least we could finish the wall painting now the carpenter's work was completed, and we all set to work, including Elizabeth Kuenzler, who had turned up before breakfast with her father. Papa said he had no intention of painting some silly wall. Instead he borrowed my paint box and whipped up three highly colored scenes. I remember one, a nude woman in the watery bower of some dark and jungly lake. He and Elizabeth were on their way to Nairobi where Elizabeth would be left. She was very unhappy about this, but Papa said "Too much in the bush is not good for a pretty girl. You must finish being educated and not stay with an old man like me all the time." He kept asking me if I was happy. "Good, good," he said. "The love is wonderful!" (This to Elizabeth, aged fourteen.) He told Andrew, "A woman is like a pressure lamp. You must heat her up before she will burn."

Later we all went over to Seronera where the new safari lodge had been finished, and found a couple there, the Milottes, who were making a film for Disney on the African lion. Their professional methods were certainly a contrast to Ansti's. Like us, they had two vehicles, one of them a Dodge Power Wagon, but the resemblances stopped there. Their power wagon had an air-conditioned and intricately fitted back on it built to their professional specifications, with sliding windows along the sides. On each side, a movie camera with a 16 inch telephoto lens was attached to the underside of a counter top and could be swung up into position (like the old Singer sewing machines) when needed. There were fitted compartments everywhere for other equipment, two folding bunks and a small stove. They could thus live in this vehicle, park it anywhere they wanted to, and wait for their opportunities. We gathered that waiting was their chief technique and a very successful one too, judging by the films they had already made: (*Seal Island* and *Bear Country*). They were devoting three years to *The African Lion*; we were meeting them on their second tour. Kindly people, too: when they heard Pru's and my plans for our Kenya visits involving ferries and buses, they offered to carry the bed rolls back to Nairobi for us, which was a great help. Physically they were both short, round, compact people. They reminded me of Mr. and Mrs. Noah in *Mary Poppins*, wheeling around on their wooden bases handing out special Conversation Pieces to all their guests.

Back at Banagi we found that more uninvited guests had arrived, so Pru and I stopped worrying about being there. "People seem to think this is a ruddy hotel," said Andrew, "in spite of Seronera."

We left for Musoma and the ferry by the end of October. In the Musoma hotel we met a man called Carl who said he'd been to the Mara with Anstruther Carapace just the week before. "Poor old guy. Crazy!" But Carl revealed that even in the game-filled Mara Ansti had missed all the good shots he could have got.

The ferry was late docking in Kisumu but we still caught the bus to Eldoret and were picked up by chance on the road by one of the Waldron's neighbors who delivered us to their door. We now embarked on a new experience: how the white man lived in the Kenya highlands in 1953. It was with an elegance and degree of comfort we found it hard, at first, to adjust to. We felt very "bush." We had no tennis clothes, and no long dresses for the evenings, and our khakis looked very out of place. A multitude of well-trained servants did everything, even running the baths; sleek horses appeared every morning with their syces, ready for anyone who cared to ride. There were fresh flowers in every room, and a full-scale tea every afternoon. Well, we were used to the idea of high tea by now, but not with so much well-polished silver. We may both have been raised respectably enough in New York, but here we felt like country mice, though we decided it was a life one could easily get used to. Our mothers would have approved of the whole set up. The Waldrons passed us on, in the easy-going East African way, to a similarly luxurious household near Nanyuki, before it was time to get back to Nairobi and the old Avenue Hotel again, and to find Ansti. This proved to be easy: he emerged from some recess the minute we arrived. "Oh how glad I am to see you," he cried with his hands held over his head. At once he offered us his car and said he'd give us $10,000 if we'd come back to him. The people standing around followed this conversation with great interest. We said we'd discuss things later. At dinner, Ansti pushed the fish around his plate as usual and spat out mouthfuls of it. Nothing had changed. But he really did seem to want us back, first to go to Carr Hartley's again and then to go on another safari he had not yet planned.

The next day we paid a duty call on the American Consul to explain things (more or less) then, having had a message from them, to the Milotte's much nicer hotel (the Norfolk) to pick up our bed rolls, Ansti's bed rolls, value $30, that he had already asked anxiously about.

Gwen in her black dress

We invited the Milottes back to tea at the Avenue where they then had the pleasure of meeting Ansti for the first time. He spared them little, but even for him seemed ill at ease, as though he was waiting for something, or someone. No one could have been more surprised than we were when in walked the girl of the photograph, the glamorous starlet Gwen, in a fluffy black dress and high heels, looking very expensive altogether. Mr. Milotte at once declared he was staying right here in Africa if Gwen was, and Ansti shot him a look of disfavor.

Why did Ansti want us back when he had this starlet up his sleeve? "We should have got that $10,000 in writing," said Pru. By then Pru had almost decided to sail back to Europe with Oliver (who was going on leave) in early December. Ansti helped her along by telling us that, with Gwen, he certainly would not want us for the Red Sea, which disappointed only me; I now had to think seriously about what I would do in a month's time. Andrew had suggested spending Christmas on the Kenya coast somehow, but all plans were up in the air. After discussing the variables, including a provisional plan to rent Oliver's land rover so we would have transport of our own if Pru did not leave with him, we decided to postpone deciding anything for the time being and to go along to Carr Hartley's with Ansti. It was still a paid job. There was no further mention of cars or large sums of money, but with an end in sight, Pru didn't object too strongly. Ansti had declared that the end date of our "contract" with him was November 30th .Where did he get this from? As it fitted in with Pru's possible plans, however, we did not demur. We could hardly complain if Ansti had got a replacement for us when we'd been "fired" and had then "disappeared."

While we were still in Nairobi, on Andrew's instructions we phoned his brother Ronald, then managing a coffee plantation in nearby Thika. He sounded charming, more "worldly" than Andrew, whatever that meant. More "sociable" perhaps. He at once invited us to dinner at his *shamba*, saying we were not to even *look* at the house or furniture as none of it was his. His other guests would pick us up and drive us back; it was no bother. Ronald proved to be precise, rather guarded, a little fussy. He was equally good-looking but so completely different from Andrew in character that I could hardly take them for brothers. Andrew had told me they did not get along very well, and I could see why.

Of course with Ansti if one ever got near making any sort of plan he was sure to change his mind. We were back on daily departure notice and daily postponements. He also announced that he had decided after all that he did want me for the Red Sea—maybe. What about Gwen? After a day or so, a note came. It said: "Miss Randall is to be regarded as my personal companion.. This safari (until November 30th) is primarily to finish P's part, but I may shoot GR as well." We were to go to Carr Hartley's, he continued, and then to Uganda, where we would "shoot innocent crocs and hippos." He said he had now decided that the Jungle Night was to be P's part and the Red Sea mine; we had few illusions about being allowed in the same frame as the glamorous Gwen.

The November "short rains" started, further messing up plans. Ansti said he might go straight to the Northwest Frontier District (dryer) instead of Uganda, or, in the opposite direction, to Lake Rukwa in southern Tanganyika. Or maybe straight to Ethiopia. Lake Rukwa was 900 miles to the southwest and supposedly filled with hippo. Lake Rudolf (300 more difficult miles to the north) had crocs. Ethiopia? Ansti had no idea what the possibilities for Jungle Nighting in Ethiopia might be, nor did we, but, well, it was more or less on the way to the Red Sea. Uganda's fresh water wildlife, "innocent" or not, now appeared to be out of the running. The possible destinations were still being debated by my birthday (November 11th); we had not yet got to Carr Hartley's. On the 11th, Ansti realized that if we wanted to go to Ethiopia we'd all need visas. The Ethiopians take their time about issuing such things. Departure was again put off so we could all go to the office of Ethiopian Airways, alias the Consulate. Pru and I, arriving after Ansti, found our employer on his knees, his papers spread around him on the floor, and Gwen seated at a borrowed typewriter trying to translate Ansti's handwriting. The man whose office this was had been forced away from his desk and into a corner. Warily, he asked there was something he could do for us. When we said we were of the floor party, he disappeared.

The extra day's delay at least gave me the chance to take my own typewriter to be repaired. I did not see it again until December.

We actually left for Thomson's Falls and Carr Hartley's place on the 12th. When we reached the farm, both Carr Hartley and his wife were "away." No one knew where they were or when they'd be back; CH had left a man called Taylor in charge. The weather now really closed in. Over the next few days it rained steadily, doggedly, all day and all night with only very small short breaks. There was one the first morning. "Into your clothes, girls," Ansti shouted; we all piled into the car in safari kit and raced down the road to a "camp site" where Ansti had got Taylor to set up a tent so he could film "camp scenes" using pairs of girls—Gwen and Pru, Pru and me, Gwen and me, covering his various options, until the rain came on again. Gwen was an old hand at this "scene" business; she was kind and generous with her advice, too; she must have thought us deplorably casual about being photographed. We all bunked together so we had plenty of chance to see the preparations necessary to appear in a film. She spent over half an hour each morning on her face ("just the basics") before she got to the make up stage, and applied new nail polish every day. Her sleek blond shoulder bob was of course curled nightly. She never appeared without either a cap or a scarf, a windbreaker over a smart blouse (white), and "frontier" pants of the sort Ansti said we could not wear because we'd get too dirty in them. Gwen never got dirty of course. She also wore a wide leather belt and leather chaplets or leggings to keep the frontier pants neatly tucked into her socks. Three pairs of socks: first, thin white ones because she had developed blisters walking around Nairobi in her high heels, then a pair of white wool socks which tied at the top around the pant legs, then brown wool socks so nothing white would show between leggings and shoe. Naturally all this could not be done in five minutes, but once finished she remained camera-ready all day, whereas we had to tidy up in a hurry whenever the weather cleared.

By the third day, even Gwen's professional calm was wearing thin. Two nights away from the comforts of hotel life (even Avenue Hotel life), she began to complain bitterly. It was still raining hard, and there was no hot water, Carr Hartley had still not come back and Taylor, who was a well-driller by profession, said he was just "helping out" and had no orders about what we might do or not do with CH's animals. To pass the time, Ansti kept trying to get Gwen to himself, but she stuck like glue with us. She remarked that Ansti shouldn't read books like *Nana* as it "gave him ideas." He still appeared to be only halfway through it.

By the afternoon, however, there was distraction aplenty. The place was buzzing. A lot of police had arrived, some of them by helicopter. Tall thin white policemen, short fat ones, and a truckload of native *askaris*. The latter spread out around the cabins while the former herded us all into one room for a "briefing." Mau Mau in the area, they announced. We got information — planning to burn down the buildings — let all the animals out. Also, a *toto*'s been killed (an African child). "Cut up in pieces and strung in a tree like these gangs usually do." The white police then drove off somewhere leaving us with some of the askaris.

Gwen became very nervous. She said she only learnt to be afraid a few years ago, but she sure was afraid now. To reassure her, Mr. Taylor lent us a revolver. It appeared to be unloaded. I remarked as much to Gwen later in our cabin, saying it was probably just to make us feel better. Gwen picked up the gun, cocked it and pressed the trigger. There was a tremendous noise and a bullet through the wall. The askaris rushed around. We were very embarrassed. All the next day we dutifully carried this gun (unloaded) around with us. Ansti could accomplish even less now with the Mau Mau around; certainly no jungle nighting. Not surprisingly he became more and more mournful: He even wondered why he hadn't shot camp scenes earlier "when we had all those tents and boys around" (dry, sunny camp scenes too). Why indeed. If we couldn't do anything, why didn't we leave? He said he was waiting for Carr Hartley to come back "to do night work with eland."

Gwen told us more about her time with Ansti before we showed up. She said she had been very polite at first, even sympathetic until he tried to spend all his spare time in her room watching her do her hair and so on. "Poor old codger," she said. She said she had felt really sorry for him at first. She said she understood how hard it was for man to be without a woman. Besides he'd told her all about us, complaining about everything and what a hard time we'd given him and what a beautiful figure I had and how he was afraid I'd marry some oaf, what a waste and how he'd never forgive himself and so on. But she soon discovered how jealous he was because he kept making comments on any male friends she made. "A Colonel just talked to me once, and right away Ansti told me I had to beware of people in hotels. Lots of fakes around, calling themselves Colonel or something," and he kept trying to put their relations on a more personal level. "I don't want you to touch me, Anstruther," she finally told him. "I can look, can't I?" he answered. "Well," said Gwen to us, "I've been modeling for years, and I'm used to people looking at me, so I couldn't say much to *that*." In Gwen's now hardened opinion, Pru and I had been much too soft with him. She wasn't going to cook any wildfowl over campfires or sleep in the open. But Gwen was not burdened with funny ideas about seeing Africa or living in the bush the way we were.

Day four at Carr Hartley's the sun came out and we all got on parade only to find Taylor had dismantled the soggy tent; As Ansti had to pay (again) to have it set back up, he decided he might as well film the process. The sun may have been out, but it was freezing cold as we sloshed around in the mud and as soon as it started to rain again, everyone disappeared back to the huts. Here, we found Carr Hartley had breezed in with some officers in the K.A.R. (King's African Rifles), locally born, full of the Mau Mau operations they'd been on —"up to our necks in it." One of them had been in the K.A.R. since 1937. The war years had been really good, he told us. "There were only about 400 of us and we won a couple of V-C's. But discipline's all gone to the dogs now. The youths that join these days just couldn't care less how they turn out, and they're pretty brutal with the Kukes too."

Like all the locally born whites, he said, they had great friends among the "Kukes" and spoke several of the tribal languages, but he thought the bad blood now between the settlers and the Kikuyu was getting so serious that if the slaughter on both sides didn't stop the other tribes might get dragged in, "the real warriors, like the Nande and Kipsigis" and then there'd be trouble. And as for lack of discipline and training, in his opinion the Home Guard were ten times worse than the Army for engendering hatred between the races. Some of the violence these young farm boys boasted about certainly made us wonder. If there were captives who needed a little roughing up to start talking, they said they did it in the early morning "before some big blowhard rolls up and wants to run the whole show. We're the only ones who keep a bit of order out Mkule way..." These people were a very different sort from the settlers we'd met at Kitale, and more interesting as a result, from my point of view. Maybe that's why Robert Ruark had concentrated on them in his book, *Uhuru*.

Ansti wandered in at sat down with his head in his hands, only to get up restlessly. He'd mislaid his wallet and his glasses, he said, and drifted out.

Carr Hartley then got an eyeful of Gwen. "It's so cold here," Gwen said plaintively and CH at once offered to warm her up. More people came in, CH's sister and brother among them, and were introduced all round. "These people are supposed to be filming here," CH explained.

"Filluming what?" asked the sister,

"Raindrops! Haven't you heard that song?"

CH got hold of Gwen's wool and held it for her. "Darling, what's that thing you're making? I need a new floor mat for my car. Can I have that thing you're making?" (Laughter)

"It's going to look very nice," Gwen said defiantly." It will look real good with black. Then I'm going to make a white stole but that will have to wait for the boat." Ansti was at this point planning to send Gwen home by boat.

"But darling what kind of boat do you think you'll be on? It'll be a cargo boat, I'll bet. Soot flying around."

Mrs. CH came in. "Someone let my pet bush baby die around here!"

CH: "What do you want me to do? You probably squeezed its stomach too hard." She went out. "Poor old thing. She gets migraine, you know."

"I'm still cold," said Gwen.

"Well I offered to warm you up. What more can I do?"

"Gwen's my girl friend, isn't she?" he said to me later.

"She's Ansti's too," I warned him. "You'd better watch out."

"Me? I'm not afraid of any man, little or that high" (gesturing towards the rafters). "Only women. There goes mine tight now," he said, following with his eyes the bedraggled form of his wife. "Poor old girl."

At breakfast the next morning, Ansti sat and bit his nails. None of us were in a good temper, Gwen having used the only hot water we'd seen for four days to wash her hair. CH suddenly turned to Pru and said, "You know, I think you've gained twenty pounds since I last saw you!" She looked at him furiously. "Only teasing," he said into the silence. "What's the matter? Don't like being teased?" She ignored him, but he didn't notice. One of the cheetah kittens (very smelly) they kept in the house had shat on his toe.

Like quite a few people we met in East Africa, CH seemed to enjoy playing a caricature of himself: the sexy redneck, the animal tamer, the behind-the-scenes prop man who made most of the so-called wildlife shots possible. I guessed he thought Hollywood could hardly function in Africa without him, and indeed he had no shortage of clients, though we found that most of them stayed in the hotel at Thomson's Falls and only came here to film and only when the weather was good. Rumuruti, the nearest village, had shops but no hotel. It was 6,200 feet above sea level and there were quite a few European owned farms in this part of the so-called "white highlands" It was west of the most troubled places like the Aberdares and the slopes of Mt. Kenya. "I tell you, sweetheart," CH said, "I really am expecting trouble around here. They burned one of my kraals before, but those bastards better be thinking twice before coming to my place again. We'll give them everything we've got. It's those farmers who say, 'Oh they'll never attack me. I've been here forty years and always looked after them'—all that rot. They're the ones who get chopped up. And their wives. No guns. 'We trust our people.' Ha ha. First they find their cattle hamstrung, then their pets hung from the farm gate. That's how it starts. No use talking of getting along. This is a war, sweetheart, you'd better believe it. You got to be tough. And strong. And here's this guy [Ansti] thinking he can run around the bush at night taking pictures of his girls netting animals? Crazy!"

"Tell him so," I said. "Tell him you won't help him. Let us all go somewhere else."

"You tell him, sweetheart. He's your boss. Me? He wants to pay to sit in my house I'm going to throw him out? Not likely. Rain, he pays. Tent up. He pays. Tent down, he pays. Food, he pays. We're not so busy now. I got a lot of animals to feed. I should throw you all out?"

Poor Ansti. But if I urged him to go back to Tanganyika he'd suspect my motives and get angry again. Right now he seemed calm, if understandably depressed. There had been no fits of the shakes. He had chosen to come here.

The very next night, with dryer weather, CH relented and did help out providing we could finish by seven, his curfew hour for his boys. Ansti had a list of wants, starting with lions. Gwen declared right away that she was not throwing any nets over lions, so Pru and I got the job, one to throw, one to leap and (supposedly) hold, at least long enough for a shot. Gwen drove and Ansti filmed, shouting instructions from the top of the truck. The young lions were dragged unwillingly into the spotlight by CH's boys at the end of a zebra leg, snarling and growling with annoyance. Pru, the appointed net-thrower, missed three times; each time the lions would have to be maneuvered back into the light with much snarling, and the boys kept out of the light. Naturally the minute the boys let go of the zebra the lions rushed off with it back to their pen and we'd have to start all over again. The camera jammed several times, but we were all, except Gwen, used to that.

Next we tried the eland. This was not a success either. As soon as we'd got the truck into the camouflaged kraal and the gates shut, the terrified eland began rushing around throwing itself at the barriers breaking off the camouflage and no one could do anything with it. CH himself got up on the truck and tried to lasso it but failed, which put him in a foul temper.

We moved on to the hippo. These were said to be very young, but even young ones weigh about 400 pounds. We were still supposed to be scientists studying animals at night, but I don't think we looked very scientific trying to hold a net down on 400 pounds of frightened hippo. I suppose Ansti got shots of "girl scientists" lying struggling in the dirt and maybe this was what Ansti had really wanted all along. We had to admit we certainly had more access to large animals here, however artificial, than we had had in a month of pleasant safari time with our game rangers. That evening, he told Gwen he didn't mind about her not netting lions but he certainly expected her to ride on top of a manta ray in the Red Sea.

"Don't be so ridiculous!" she said.

After supper, CH entertained us with anecdotes about the N.F.D., one of the places Ansti said he might go next. He had lots of stories about the wild Turkana on the shores of Lake Rudolf and had been on the arduous track to Ethiopia Ansti talked of taking, He stressed the terrible lack of water.

"Water! Beware the man who has no water! He'll kill you for what you've got."

The places to find water were: inside a baobab (at the bottom), or in green palm nuts if you could find any. The wells were often foul or barred by tribesmen "who'd cut off your balls as soon as look at you—pardon me, girls." He said he'd been without water once, lay under a tree a whole day before he was rescued, his tongue black and swollen, stuck to the roof of his mouth. "Never try to drink the sap in the sansovera, though—even though elephant do. That stuff can kill a man." Gwen soon tired of this conversation and went to bed. So did we. We were said to be leaving the next day.

When we got to the Avenue, the first person we saw was Elizabeth Kuenzler looking miserable behind the reception desk. When she managed to get away from her work, she came to our room with her tale of woe. We had never thought much of the management of the hotel, in the hands of a French couple from India, and they were proving very unkind to this young girl who was only supposed to work part time for them in return for board while she finished her schooling. They told her father she'd room with their daughter, but now they said they didn't want her anywhere near them. She wasn't allowed to eat with them, and it was do this, do that all day long until she was locked in her little garret room at 8:30 in the evening. Poor Elizabeth! And her father had gone back to the bush thinking she was well looked after. We offered to try to find her another place to live, but she said she'd better stay where he put her. So we wrote a long letter to Papa K. care of Mr. Metz in Ikoma, very strongly put, but couldn't do more: we really were leaving the next day—for Lake Rukwa. Tanganyika after all.

Gwen had a tale to tell in the morning. We were eating breakfast together, unhampered by Ansti's presence. She said, now that Ansti had us back he was dying to get rid of us because we cramped his style. He was making constant advances to her. We were lucky, she said, that we hadn't had to put up with that sort of thing. He'd also said a lot more about us, accusing us of lewd behavior, living in sin and so on, but that was nothing new. Ansti joined us. In silence we watched him pushing his food around.

"Part of the spotlight's been left in Namanga," he announced. "That's two whole days wasted if I go back to get it."

"It's nothing of the sort," I said. "We can make a detour to pick it up on the way."

Ansti ignored me. "I need one girl to go with me," he said cannily. "What if I get stuck there and think I have three assistants sitting in a hotel doing nothing? That's my train of thought."

After a grim silence, I volunteered, but it was quite clear he wanted Gwen who, on some pretext, had left the table. "Go after her, Wendy. Tell her it's a very scenic route. She can see Kilimanjaro." I relayed this message and Gwen's reply as neutrally as I could. What she actually said was "No thank you. I've had enough."

Ansti and I had a silent trip. Still, one might as well try. As we were then passing Longido, I said "That's a famous rock."

"Oh? Why?" said Ansti, straining to see it out of my window.

"A battle was fought on the plains here between the English and Germans. The Germans put up very stiff resistance at Longido." I had got this from Andrew.

"The Germans kept the natives in their place," said Ansti. "Whip technique."

Nothing more was said until we got to Namanga and found the missing piece of the spotlight still sitting on the driveway. No one had thought to move it, or maybe even noticed it. The hotel was silent in the heat of midday and no one noticed us either as we drove in and out again. We got a flat tire on the way back, the second in two days I noted.

Lake Rukwa

At departure time the next morning, Oliver turned up just as we were coming down the stairs with our bags. Pru had all of ten minutes with him before Ansti appeared, shouting at the boys and giving one of them ten shillings and telling him to divide it, a method of tipping which never failed to cause chaos. In the rumpus, Oliver winked at us and made off without being seen.

Baobabs, S. Tanganyika

Gwen soon realized that a little trip to Rumuruti had not prepared her for the full horror of safari life with Ansti. She stood it remarkably well, considering everything. She started out in the power wagon, but soon insisted she was being bumped too much, so joined me in the station wagon. I was driving and as she sat chatting beside me I learned a lot about her and her life.

"I had a husband, once, like Ansti," she said. "When I was twenty-one. That's why I can handle him so well — I know his type. I had a little boy by him too. I worry about him. His name's Jimmy. That's why I'm here. I want to earn enough money so I can have him with me. He's with my ex's parents now and if I leave him there long they'll turn him against me. They're so possessive they'll hardly let him come to see me.

You see, Wendy, the trouble was, between his father and me, we were both too young when we got married. He was absolutely ruled by that mother of his. We were in Hollywood at the time, but after I'd had the baby we moved to New York and got a small apartment. I guess we were never very happy together. I had had a lot of trouble having the kid, and I should have had post-surgery but the doctor didn't care. I got an infection and then I had to have an operation, and after that he had to be careful of me, see, but he didn't like that. He was a bit of a sadist, I think, and I think sometimes he really wanted to hurt me.

"Sometimes I think he only married me to show his mother that he *could* have everything he wanted, and then he used to shout at me and be mean to me to show I hadn't got anything on him either. He was a mixed-up kid, as they say. I guess I've always liked to analyze people. I guess I'm lucky that way. It lets me sort of get outside myself and see things clearly. Like Ansti for instance. I knew what he'd be like, right away, from his letter. And I knew what the trip would be like, right from the start. I just knew, that's all. Nothing can surprise me any more, because I just know. I like reading philosophy sometimes because I find it so restful. I just know there too. That's why I never can understand why everyone goes around making out like philosophy's so difficult. I just seem to get inside it and feel it, and it's all clear as day."

I could think of no suitable comment. So I said, in order to lead her back to Hollywood and her life there, "I've always been sorry I couldn't act — what does it feel like to be good at it?"

"Oh, you're lucky, Wendy! I've always been sorry I could act so well! You go about living in a dream world, you see, and you get emotional fulfillment but nothing else. I lived in Hollywood again after my divorce — and I got married again, by the way — but he was peculiar too. I attract that type, I think. Ten years in Hollywood and nothing but peculiar people around me. It must have affected me. It's all because I can handle them so well. In Hollywood, after I'd finally bust up with my ex they thought I was a perfect angel about everything. 'She's so sweet,' I heard people saying. 'I hope she doesn't lose it.' Well, I held out for ten years, but by last year it was beginning to get me down. Some pretty handsome men used to chase me — I had quite a few affairs, I guess — all kinds. For instance there was this guy I worked for once — I was just crazy about him. We used to go out together all the time, but it became too hard on me. It interfered with the work, you might say, because I just couldn't look at him without loving him and the whole staff knew about it pretty soon and I couldn't stand that, everybody knowing, so I left and I wouldn't go back. He pled with me to go back, but I told him no, I wanted him too much to work for him. He was married, you see...then there was Joe. He lived in New York. He's a foreigner. Italian, I guess. Anyway I stay at his apartment whenever I go to New York even now, and he's so gallant he doesn't even touch me. He's a little fellow, very foreign-looking. Once we went to the theater — he takes me out all the time, and I feel like a heel because he's doing it all for nothing as it were — I mean I enjoy being with him and all that, but I don't — I wouldn't have an affair with him and I'm sort of embarrassed to go out with him and that makes me feel like a heel too."

This train of thought was interrupted rudely by yet another flat tire. Ansti had just got out of sight ahead of us, having passed us because he said his lights were failing and he wanted to have someone behind him. It was a black night, illumined by a new moon but no stars. I got out.

"What do we do now?" asked Gwen.

"We change the tire," I said, perhaps a little crisply. I got out the jack. It was filthy. I couldn't seem to make it work either, not having used it before, so while I thought about it, I tried to undo the nuts on the wheel. I soon decided this must be one of the tires not recently changed: the nuts seemed immovable.

"Ansti will come back for us when he sees were not there, won't he?" said Gwen.

"Not if his lights aren't working," I said. I had little faith that Ansti would even notice our absence for a long time. I tried the nuts again. Gwen stood over me, clucking sympathetically. Finally I suggested we try to drive on for a bit, hoping the soft sand of the road would mean less tire damage. We did, but then the radiator started hissing. By then we were sick of the struggle to open the stiffly hinged back to get at things, so we decided to put the drinking water left in Ansti's flask in the radiator. Just then, lights and the power wagon roared up Ansti got out demanding to know what the hell we were doing, then he saw his flask in my hand and the radiator cap in Gwen's and flew at us again for using his drinking water. Why was he in such a temper? We weren't slow to answer back. Ansti then changed the tire, misplacing nut after nut in the sand in his usual way.

We got going again, the Weak Sister in front. Both of us were told to look for his lights and stop at once if we didn't see them. I assured Gwen I could do this in the rear view mirror. She said her back was hurting.

"I have a friend in Hollywood, Wendy. Her name is Gail and she really is the craziest kid, 'cause each fellow she meets she swears is The Man, the love of her life, then I see her a week later and it's somebody else. I can sympathize because it used to be like that for me too, but now I've learned. I want security, now, and affection, and a home for Jimmy. Last year I met just the man for me, a Texas oil man, the nicest man I'd ever met — real normal! He really loved me, not just my figure like some of the others. He was blond, twenty-eight years old, just right — but he was married, you see, with three children, and his wife — they didn't love each other or anything, but he was too fond of his children to make a stand — what a mess. He treated me like an angel! I was never his mistress, you know, but it was making both of us so unhappy I knew I had to get away from it all. Then this job came up so I took it. My in-laws live in Texas too, and if they had found out I was having an affair with a married man — well, they're down enough on me already. I tell you, Wendy, I'm not interested in men on this trip at all, but I can't make Ansti understand that. You know what he said to me? 'We must find Wendy a boy friend in the Red Sea.' We, indeed. You're a good kid, don't let anyone louse up your life…I'm going to start all over again when I get over this last one. No more married men for me. I think I should be about recovered by the time we get to the Red Sea — that's the part Ansti really hired me for, you know — that's what I like doing, all that swimming. Gee, I wish my back hadn't gone. It must be my kidneys. All this jouncing around. I thought I had sleeping sickness once…"

I never did find out why Gwen thought she had sleeping sickness because at that moment we arrived in Singida and drew up outside what passes for a hotel there. It had a façade and a sort of reception place, but behind this was a dank courtyard beyond which there were a few small rooms, and beyond that, Africa. Ansti said we ought to go to the government rest house, but Gwen said she was sick and not going anywhere and he shouldn't be so silly. Then they all declared that they were not hungry. Not hungry? I was ravenous. I wheedled the proprietor into making us some sandwiches and noticed when they came, that I was not eating them alone.

"I was sick all last night," said Gwen plaintively in the morning. "Nothing worse than feeling your kidneys on a trip like this."

We changed driving arrangements, Pru and Gwen in the station wagon. When we stopped at Itigi, Pru reported that Gwen hadn't said a word the whole way. Ansti allowed us to have lunch at the "Dak Refreshment House, Number 18" and Gwen indeed was the picture of unhappiness. Out loud, she day-dreamed of soft beds and cleanliness. Pru and I went for a walk. Itigi was a larger place than Singida, but very regimented. All the houses were made of concrete, low and square and numbered. Even the birds that flew low over our heads perched in short-trunked flamboyant trees placed at regular intervals around the main square. Ansti, messing around with the vehicles in the drive, stopped me on my way in.

"What do you think about Gwen? Is she really sick? She could sue me! And I know what hospital bills can come to."

I looked at him. He really was worried, if mostly about money. "Leave it until Lake Rukwa and see how she is there," I suggested. "She's not used to African roads."

We had company for lunch: a railroad man, a missionary and a man with a hare lip. Just as the food was brought in, Ansti went out slamming the door behind him. "How far are you going?" asked Railroad. "You'd better carry all your petrol with you," advised Hare lip lugubriously. Ansti came back, through another door and slammed that too. There were cries of protest as this shut off all the air circulation. "How far is Chunya?" he asked. Chunya was the next town of any size, just beyond our turn off at Mkongolosi for Lake Rukwa. Railroad said it was 250 miles. "I thought it was 160," said Ansti suspiciously. "We could camp out. Yeah, guess that's what we gotta do, girls," he said with one of those funny grins of his. "Hope you feel well, Gwen," he added, "the worst is yet to come." He positively leered at this. We all maintained a rigid silence.

"Have you found it interesting out here?" the missionary enquired of Ansti in a soft voice.

"Yes. Interesting," said Ansti in a monotone.

"It's only worth shooting a tommy, in my mind," said Hare Lip who worked for the Tanganyika meat packers. "If you go out after elephant or buffalo, it's just a waste of ammo and time."

"Had a good time in the Belgian Congo," Ansti volunteered.

"I'm glad of that," said the missionary. "A good many of my brethren are there, I believe."

"Stayed a lot with the Black Papas," Ansti continued. "Gave me a lot of stuff. Ate with them and the Black Mamas a lot." We shut our eyes in embarrassment. The missionary looked down at his plate. The "fish course" had been cleared away, and some sort of meat with cabbage and potatoes was served. Chickens wandered in and out of the open door and I thought how nice it would have been to have had one of them. One is never grateful for one's blessings, I said to myself severely, the influence of the missionary perhaps. For such a thin man, he was putting away an amazing amount of food.

"No trouble here, do they?" asked Hare lip.

"Up to now," conceded Railroad, "but we're expecting it. With the warning Kenya has given us, we're tightening up consid'ably. Believe some Mau Mau started north of Arusha…"

"It's queer country around here," said Hare lip.

The waiter, a Goan, had gathered up the plates. "I am sorry for the pudding," he announced. "It will be perhaps a little late."

"Not so many people here," said Pru.

"That's true," said Hare lip generously. "I like Tanganyika though. More friendly atmosphere, don't you think?" This last was addressed to Ansti.

"Yeah," Ansti said. He was busy trying to get a piece of meat out from between his teeth.

The missionary gazed out the only window at the sand-colored landscape.

"How did you come here?" Hare lip asked Ansti, evidently bothered by silences.

"Through the Congo," said Ansti. "I came through the Congo," he repeated, having removed his fingers from his mouth. He had a far away look on his face. "I liked Gabon, in the summertime."

"Congo, did you say?" Railroad had been out and come back. "I always think it's hard to tell one bit of forest from another!" He laughed cordially. Ansti looked through him.

The pudding arrived. It was one of those incredible British things made out of bits of bread and bright yellow Bird's Custard Powder, very liquid.

"In such things as road travel," continued Railroad undeterred, "I understand the Congo is much better than here."

"Roads very narrow," said Ansti.

We all moved into the lounge for coffee.

"I wish we were there already," said Gwen, not referring to the Congo.

"I doubt if we get there today," from Pru.

"Best thing to do," said Ansti, overhearing this, "is to camp by the road. Better get going before it gets dark."

Hare lip's colleague whom he said he was expecting now joined us. He had dark wavy hair. He looked appreciatively at Gwen. "Of course you could all stay right here for the night," he suggested smoothly.

"Happy thought," said Gwen.

"We're going down south tomorrow," said Wavy Hair. "Starting about 4 A.M," added Hare lip. "Oh if we leave at 8 it will be all right," said Wavy, still looking at Gwen. I noticed that Gwen was indeed rather pale.

"Better get that drum of gas," Ansti announced and went out.

As usual, the men began to discuss Africa and the Africans between themselves. They were all against the clever educated African, claiming they misdirected their education towards crime or Mau Mau activities. They all believed in a Firm Hand. "When the African finds the land getting built up around him and he has to get a job and work, that's when you start getting trouble. They look back to good old days when there was plenty of land and their women did all the work. That's when it starts. Of course it's better in Tanganyika—no white settlers here."

Pru said that she found the attitude of the Kenya farmers simply barbarous and recounted some of the rougher tales about the treatment meted out to the Mau Mau when they were caught which we'd heard at Carr Hartley's.

"Mind you," said Wavy, "they've had the provocation."

"It seems," said the missionary who was picking up his bags, "that there's a better understanding between us and our black brothers here in Tanganyika. We try to do our best towards it, I know." There was a murmur of agreement. He paid his bill and went out into the shadeless afternoon. Tanganyika Territory was under U.N. mandate.

Ansti had still not returned. As Wavy went out the door, he said "I still think the best plan is to stay the night."

I said, "There's an American expression: tell it to the Marines."

"Right," said Hare lip. "No more said. But I still think it's best to start at four in the morning," and he too drifted out.

"If Ansti would only tell us what we're supposed to be doing, we could be doing it," said Gwen.

When Ansti returned, we tackled him. "Gwen isn't well. Why don't we let her rest and then leave at four in the morning?"

"No point in getting up in the dark," said Ansti. "Can't see. Lose everything."

"Well if you're incapable—" from Pru who was once again thoroughly fed up with Ansti.

"No excitement here, I guess," countered Ansti slyly.

"You ought to be glad to have us all to yourself," I remarked.

"Wait 'til you get up on the Northern Frontier," Ansti said to Gwen with that awful smile. "400 miles between hotels. Can't get breakfast if you leave at that hour," he added.

The waiter had just come back into the room. "Can we get breakfast about 5 AM tomorrow?" Gwen asked him.

"Yes, Madam, I will be here at that time."

Silence and the biting of nails. Gwen had buried herself in an old Reader's Digest. Pru said, determinedly, "So when shall we all be called?

More silence.

Ansti, (deciding to stay): "Well if you're really sick Gwen, I guess we'll have to stay…"

Gwen promptly went to bed. Pru and I washed some clothes outside the room so as not to disturb her, but she kept calling us with small requests. She didn't want the Africans to come into the room, she said. By beer time, we escaped and went downstairs only to be called back. Gwen wanted hot toddy. Ansti, hearing this, demanded a half bottle of whisky from the bar and tucking it into the back pocket of his greasy shorts insisted on ministering to her himself. A different collection of itinerants except for the same railroad man had assembled for dinner. They watched Ansti going back and forth with some curiosity. Dinner itself was interrupted several times by requests from Gwen who now wanted sustenance. She must be getting better, I thought. But when we went up to collect the trays she had collapsed back into fitful slumber. "I really should not have woken myself up to eat," she murmured faintly.

By the time we came back upstairs to go to bed, she was wide awake. "Oh I am so bored," she said, but we were past caring and went to sleep.

We were all up early and breakfasted only to find the power wagon's radiator was leaking. Ansti stomped around blaming Carr Hartley's boys for having used the wrong sized bolts. Here the railroad man was of some help, though still very garrulous. The only person he didn't bother with his endless stories was Gwen, oddly enough. Gwen had appeared fully accoutered for Safari: frontier pants, scarf around the neck, scarf around the head, cap, battle jacket, dark glasses. How did she stand it in the heat? She was also armed with her shorthand book which she sat down to study while the rest of us milled around. I made a mental note to take up shorthand. It seemed to be the only thing that kept the bores away.

This was unkind, as Railroad was being helpful and seemed genuinely concerned. "I'd have those bolts checked soon, if I were you."

"Shall we go?" said Ansti to us.

"Those bolts really need replacing altogether," said Railroad. "Now, see, I've managed to stop the leak, but for a long trip I wouldn't advise… there's nothing on the road between here and Chunya, except a rest house in about 170 miles…maybe you'd better stay another night and get a good start…"

Half the morning had already been used up. Ansti got his trapped look. Then he swiftly replaced it by a don't-think-you can-put-anything-over-on-me look. "The radiator," he announced to everyone, "only leaked from the top. So there's nothing wrong with the bolts after all."

Even Railroad was struck dumb.

By now it was lunchtime, so we had some. Gwen said she was still feeling shaky. Pru and I were assigned to the Weak Sister; Ansti said he had to have Gwen with him and she said she was too weak to argue. I drove and drove fast. I had a theory that you only hit half the bumps this way. We stopped twice, once for water and once for eggs, and got to the rest house, the usual bare two-roomed affair, at 6:15. No sign of

Ansti and Gwen. We had the food with us, but he had the camp beds. We prepared some food and waited and they finally turned up.

We were very organized the next morning, packing up and feeding everyone. Ansti ate Gwen's egg as well as his own, by mistake he said. Gwen, who didn't care about her egg but did about her clothes, now found her best ones had been liberally soaked by leaking fuel. She said a good many things to Ansti, just as we had at first, those long two months ago when we weren't as canny about where we put our stuff as we were now. She refused to go with Ansti again, so I did and had a harrowing ride. We fought over which road to take—this was normal—but then in a temper Ansti kept swerving wildly on the sandy road, and on the cliff road, when we could at last see Lake Rukwa spread out below us, he hit a huge bump at top speed and nearly went over the edge. I'm afraid I screamed, which is always a bad thing to do. Distracting.

The Bousfields were actually expecting us, which was nice. Like Carr Hartley, Jack Bousfield supplemented the income to be made from a shamba and croc hunting by providing crocs and hippos for photographic safaris. Gwen at once demanded a hot bath, not something settlers go in for in the middle of the day. She looked suitably pale, but being hot and tired ourselves we were not very solicitous. The male Bousfields all rallied around, however, and she was treated as she should be. The female family members had fine clear cut faces but bad legs and no figures. We all got along very well at lunch especially since the shandies flowed like water and we were very thirsty. I think it was all a bit hearty for Gwen, who soon retired to our little cabin saying what she really needed after such a trip was a facial and a long nap. It proved too hot to nap, though, so she spent a good hour looking at her face in the mirror of her dressing case and applying things. The hut was small and airless at that time of day and we were all bathed in sweat. The sun, sinking slowly over the water, radiated heat from the parched shores. Several of these small guest huts surrounded what the Bousfields called the Big House, which consisted mostly of one enormous room and a verandah dotted with deck and rocking chairs facing west across the lake. None of the family used the Big House at this time of year; certainly not the verandah. We had meals in a gloomy annex at a very long table, and everyone gathered for drinks in yet another house whose chief attraction was that it had mosquito netting in all the apertures.

We had shandies again and I drank as though I had been in a desert for days. So did everyone else. We discussed the heat and why the rains hadn't come. Though this was fortunate for Ansti's filming, everyone else was waiting for a break in the oppressive weather.

Jack explained where he slept in this season: on top of a spidery-legged affair, like a summer house on stilts. He said it was very cool and, taking Gwen's arm, offered to show it to her. It was quite a while before they rejoined us. Later, in our cabin, she stood moodily at the door in her nightdress, sighing. In theory we had a choice in our hut between air and mosquitoes but it was too breathless outside to make a difference.

Ansti planned to start at once with the hippo, but Jack was firm. "Give your girls some rest," he told him. Ansti said he didn't like to think of all the hippos sitting out there while his girls were sitting here, but Jack said "the hippo will stay put all right, don't worry—some of the poor things even get stuck in the mud this time of year." I guess Ansti didn't want to look like a tyrant, so he went off to potter. I overheard him later, though, warning Jack about Gwen. "She's not suited to this kind of life, you know. Sick all the way down. Sickly girl. Takes meals in her room. Has trouble with her liver."

The next day we drove to the "hippo camp." Pru went with Ansti. It was her turn, and Jack drove the station wagon with Gwen in front beside him and me in the back on the bags. It was far too hot to sit three in front. Inevitably, when I was not looking at the flat countryside, I looked at Gwen and Jack, a backstage glimpse of Hollywood in action, I thought. Since in Gwen's mind I enjoyed the position of being a good kid, she was quite uninhibited in front of me and she and Jack already seemed to be on happily familiar terms. Gwen's arm, resting on the back of his seat meant that her hand, on the rough road, often fell on the back of his neck, and there were many occasions for the pressure of full breast against manly arm. Gwen had absolutely sensational breasts, by the way. There was also the stretching of feminine body, the arranging of neat thighs, the pointing of tiny feet, the graceful arrangement of hands, and the smiles, always the smiles. And the giggle. At everything—shy, feminine, polite, admiring, sincere.

A game of twenty questions was begun, a chance to tease and for whispered consultations, real close, as Gwen would say Occasionally she turned around "to see if Ansti was coming along all right" and when she did she winked at me. I wondered how long all this would go on without some serious trouble from Ansti.

We never found out. We didn't see Gwen again until we met up in Asmara and by that time so many other things had happened I never asked her about Lake Rukwa.

Pru and I were running out of time. The day we started out after hippo was already the 25th of November, and we spent the 25th and 26th searching for them in spite of Jack's assurance that they would stay put. The second night both vehicles got stuck in black sticky mud, having ventured too near the water's edge and we all had to walk back to camp. Then it was the 27th and we, Pru and I, had to leave, she to be back in Nairobi by the 30th to pick up her boat ticket and both of us with our contract supposedly up on that day. After a lot of discussion, Ansti decided to lend us the W.S. to go back in. We reckoned to make good time (if we didn't break down) but it was still 900 miles.

Looking back, we were extraordinarily lucky the station wagon held up. It was a different story with the tires. I was now efficient with the jack, but we had a lot of punctures. Fortunately the rains held off: the road crossed several seasonal rivers. Everywhere we stopped we heard, "When will the rains come? We've never known them so late." We were only seriously held up once, on a long section of nothing but dry bush, by getting two punctures at the same time when the only spare had already been used. We sat by the side of the road considering our options. We had water, some food and fuel. It could have been worse.

After an hour, a car appeared driven by a young man with long blond hair accompanied by an elegant woman. She said she came from Philadelphia. She was so good looking that I at first thought her the blond man's wife, but she turned out to be his mother. They had just finished having the great Hemingway, in East Africa at this time, to stay and had found him a "quiet, unassuming type." They were traveling in a good car complete with tire irons and puncture repair kits, unlike us. At once the son set to work, mended the inner tubes, put everything back together and they waved us goodbye. Wonderful. We reached Mtu wa Mbu that night. Pru planned to leave all her safari stuff there against her return to Africa. She had decided to marry Oliver.

Next day, Arusha and then Nairobi. But by now Ansti's tires really were worn out. We were only a few hundred yards down the Nairobi road when we had another puncture, and twenty yards further on a blowout on the same wheel. We limped back to the Safari House. Pru wasn't feeling well anyway. The following day, rather than risking more trouble, Pru took the bus-taxi to Nairobi to collect her ticket. I sent a letter and a telegram to Ansti telling him about the punctures and adding the news that a broken spring was now tied up with rope, explaining that for these reasons and because we'd heard there had been a lot of rain on the "dry weather roads further north we might not be able to get the car as far as Nairobi as promised." In the telegram I asked him to let me know in Mombasa when he would be leaving for the N.F.D. and did he know he needed permits and passes to enter closed areas? Did he have them? Ansti was inclined to forget such things. I said we'd be in Mombasa care of Barclay's Bank until December 9th when Oliver and Prudence were due to sail.

All the Plans Change

I spent the next day idly being squired around by Tony, the blond "oily man" as Andrew called him. Andrew himself was completely out of touch and inaccessible, on the expedition to climb Oldonyo Lengai volcano with Ralph Tanner, the project they'd been planning.

When Pru got back from Nairobi, there was a farewell going on leave party for Oliver at Tangeru. Oliver did a hula-hula dance with two of the agricultural experts then fell off the bar when making a speech. Pru was toasted as his fiancée and Logan Hughes attached himself to me to tell me all about his Past. It wasn't interesting, but he seemed in need of sympathy so I tried to be sympathetic. Alan was there too, with his girlfriend, a school teacher not a scientist, out on a visit from England. I don't remember having anything to eat except bacon and eggs at three in the morning.

We made an early start for Mombasa in spite of the party, but were stopped just down the road by Mike Swettenham, owner of the Arusha garage, who told us Ansti had already been in. Mike had "not had the pleasure of" before and was an excellent mimic. Ansti's flat tones rang through the garage.

"Where's my car? Where are my girls?"

"I don't know, I don't know," Mike had kept saying. Ansti, not at all convinced, had wandered off. He returned with the car (we had left the keys at the hotel's desk) half an hour later. Mike, on looking at it, discovered that the whole chassis had been detached from the body for some time and it was probably only the loads we carried that kept it in one piece.

After leaving Mike, we stopped to get some apples for the journey and ran into Logan. At that point, he seemed to be just another impediment to getting off. To my surprise he drew me aside. "You remember last night you asked what type of girl I would fall for?" I did remember asking at the end of a long dreary recital of all the "wrong" girls in his life. He gave me a piercing look. "You," he said. His mouth quivered slightly. I tried to laugh it off, promising him a sister (I didn't have one) but he gave me another look that was pure suffering, managed a small tragic smile, and drove off. I hoped he'd forget.

We had changed vehicles but not much for the better. Oliver's old land rover had acquired bad land rover shimmy, the steering wobbling erratically whenever we hit corrugations in the lateritic dust of the road (frequent) and half way to Mombasa the fan belt broke. Oliver kept saying these things were to be expected in any land rover of a certain age. Nothing to worry about. Everything else was in perfect condition. He was very persuasive and we believed him. I was supposed to drive the thing back to Arusha by myself when he and Pru had sailed.

In Mombasa, dusty and disheveled, we got rooms and ate. Oliver and Pru went off somewhere. Not wanting to sit in the lounge by myself, I went upstairs to our hot stuffy room; it was hot and stuffy everywhere, being that time of year. I finally went to sleep. The next thing I knew, I was being shaken awake by Pru. It was about one in the morning. She was standing over me. "Are you awake? I have something very important to discuss with you."

I woke up. Pru announced that she'd just told Oliver she wasn't going to marry him. She wasn't going on the boat. It was all off. She said he didn't seem to mind and neither did she, so that was that.

Well! We still had a couple of days in Mombasa before the boat left. During this curious time, whenever I was with them, I noticed that Pru now began to find fault with Oliver over small things and even this Oliver brushed off nonchalantly. I didn't know what to make of it. I could see that my own plans, to go to South Africa and look up introductions there before meeting Andrew for Christmas, were to be thrown out. Depressing. I also got the trots, something that happened to us almost as regularly as the curse; in this case, what we called the "sick-trots" when you need to throw up as well. The farewells, such as they were, seemed very drawn out. We had to get back to Arusha and we had Oliver's boy, Shauri, to look after too. Why had he brought Shauri down to Mombasa? He was very spoiled and tried to push us around about things he said Oliver had promised him, but had not mentioned to us.

Shauri in his new hat

In Arusha, everyone seemed happy Pru now wasn't marrying Oliver and Alan told Logan Hughes that he'd decided, cautiously, that he might be a little in love with her himself. What about the school teacher? Hughes announced that he was now "eternally" in love with me and that if I married Andrew Bagnall he would leave East Africa forever. I was past caring and went to bed.

No relief the next day. We had to take Shauri back to Mtu wa Mbu, Pru said, and collect her things, but Mtu wa Mbu was now occupied by Hughes and was the last place I wanted to go. Pru seemed very tetchy about everything, not surprising, I suppose, and flew at me when I dared to criticize Shauri for his rather insolent behavior. She also said she could not bear sitting around at Mtu with Hughes knowing he was in love with me. I wasn't keen either and it was not a jolly evening trying to keep things pleasant at least on the surface. Logan could be good company, but not in his present mood. Fortunately a white hunter, Stanley Lawrence-Brown, his energetic wife and their youngest, a spotty baby named Wendy, turned up. Lawrence-Brown was full of tales of an American all-girl safari that was coming soon. He said they were to spend no less than three weeks in or near Mtu wa Mbu. This gave me great hope that Logan would fasten on someone else. Lawrence-Brown offered Pru and me jobs on this safari if we wanted them. We said we'd see.

Back in Arusha, we looked around for Ansti and Gwen, but they'd left for Nairobi. Mike was still trying to weld the chassis of the Weak Sister. We spent the next two days lotus-eating, fiddling around, dropping in on people other people knew. We went to a locally produced play and several bad movies. We annoyed Alan by stealing one of the "baboon crossing" signs and putting it near the house he was staying in. We went swimming in the lake. We were getting quite good at dropping off into the middle of the lake at the end of that long rope. We drank a lot of beer We were taken out to someone's house to ride their horses, we assumed by invitation, but no one was home except their surly cook and, in the barn, an exhausted-looking wire-haired terrier being fed upon by five unidentifiable puppies.

There always seemed to be four of us packed into the front seat of a land rover, and no one seemed to be doing any work. We went to the Riverside Inn for lunch, but no one had any. In a curtained off alcove we saw Lord Delamere's daughter lying flat on a couch, a long cigarette holder in her hand..

Logan had been muttering for a day or so about a letter he was writing me and that evening he pushed it into my hand. I went to have a bath and read it there as Pru seemed to be crying in the bedroom. The letter was quite moving in its way and gave me a very peculiar feeling. What on earth could I say? I somehow felt the whole business had little to do with me—that he had just decided on this eternal love business blindly. He knew Andrew and I were engaged and he had had no encouragement. Perhaps unrequited love was a thing with him, with its own satisfactions.

At last we left for Nairobi in Oliver's land rover, which we had rented from him. The wheel shimmy was still very much with us. Skittering around on a road without much traffic was O.K.; the scary part was trying to aim for a narrow one-track bridge. It was very hard to keep the vehicle headed right. But it didn't actually let us down until, on the outskirts of Nairobi, the clutch gave out. We caused traffic jams at every intersection and roundabout until we finally limped into a garage. The owner informed us he was not a land rover garage and had no spare parts, but we must have looked desperate. He did something, and we went on to look for a hotel. We tried the Norfolk, the nicest place. No room. We left a note for the Milottes who always stayed there, in case they came to town, and got a room at the New Stanley. We couldn't bear the thought of the Avenue again. The New Stanley, modern-looking with lots of chrome, occupied a corner at the foot of Delamere Avenue, and the contrast between its brash appearance and our possessions in their small, worn and dusty containers being carried through the main lobby and up the stairs was very marked. We felt like gypsies. How had we accumulated so much stuff?

By now it was now December 12th. We planned to spend one night in Nairobi, one night with Ronald in Thika (he had invited us) and then go on to friends of friends near Mweiga, who had also issued a casual invitation. We tried to get hold of Ronald and the friends on the telephone. Ronald turned out to have moved to a different coffee shamba and didn't answer at the new number. The Marrians at Mweiga were out too, so we went to the movies. People had told us they were afraid to walk around Nairobi at night and even in daylight, but we decided that was only because they didn't live there, like those who are terrified by New York City. We reckoned the Mau Mau concentrated on people whose guns they could steal. In any case, there had been no killings in the city lately, only robberies. We suffered a few coarse whistles from the soldiers but nothing worse.

In the morning, Pru went to the U.S. Consulate to pick up our mail while I tried to get the land rover fixed. We were determined to leave the New Stanley as soon as we could. Breakfast had been embarrassing: a room full of well-dressed tourists and waiters who did not even "see" us in our corner for a very long time. We saw only one person we thought we knew: the man who had collected us from our bus near the Waldron's, but we weren't sure. We watched him for a while and thought that he might have a hangover by the way he kept squeezing his eyes tight shut. Finally we went over to his table. He peered up at us from his newspaper, asked us what we were doing and whether we would like to have lunch with him some day. Tomorrow perhaps? We thanked him but said we were on our way to the Marrians at Mweiga. He was acquainted with the Marrians, he said, looking at us a little doubtfully.

Just as we were loading our disreputable-looking stuff back into Oliver's equally rough-looking land rover, he appeared. We could not tell him where we were going just then (in answer to his polite enquiry) but drove off, waving cheerfully only to stall in the middle of the traffic. Restarted, we waved again. He stood on the curb, returning our wave, looking mystified. For the rest of the day we were worried about running into him.

We decided to go first to the immigration office to sort out our status. On the way a large, sleek vehicle hooted and overtook us. It was Stanley Lawrence-Brown in his enormous new Chrysler, obtained, we were later told, through a very complex deal with a Mr. Hopkins, one of his American clients. "God, the people we have to take out!" he said. "But they're useful." I was surprised to hear Mr. Hopkins was not Mexican. Most of the English here who had, like the ones in Britain at this time, no legal way to obtain dollars (because of currency restrictions), seemed to find the Mexicans who came here always willing to do a deal. Stan didn't have much to say after chasing us down a side street, only that he hadn't forgotten about a possible job for us with the American All-Girl Safari, due out shortly.

The Immigration Officer, the same one Ansti had embarrassed when we first arrived, knew us all well by now, even Gwen. Nevertheless, Pru was nervous as she had not reported coming to Nairobi from Tanganyika to collect her boat ticket. Every non-British citizen or non-resident must report every crossing between Kenya and Tanganyika, and into and out of Uganda as well for all we knew, for some bureaucratic reason. But he was nice enough about it. We then did the rest of our errands and even went to the Avenue. No Ansti, no Gwen, not even Elizabeth Kuenzler. We went to the Queens to use the phone to try to reach Ronald. I went in leaving Pru trying to park outside. As soon as she had a place lined up and was about to back in, a taxi swooped into it. This happened three times. When I came out she had collected a crowd of bystanders all cheering her on and shouting at the taxis. Eventually we got the car just where we wanted her, in front of a little grill near the Queens that had quite good steaks for fifty cents. We sat right near the door so we could watch the car—there was no way to lock it. A lot of people passing looked at us curiously. Nairobi is full of shady-looking types. We were eating because we thought we ought not to go to the Norfolk to call on the Milottes without having had lunch first, in case they asked. We were full of complex scruples.

At the Norfolk we tried Ronald again. We now believed it might be impossible ever to reach him. Then we had coffee with the kindly Milottes, and after exchanging news of Banagi, lions and other things, they spoke to the manager and miraculously got us a room for the night. We collapsed into it accompanied once again by our stuff, and considered our next move. We still had not reached the Marrians to find out if they could have two girls instead of the one they were vaguely expecting, and on a different date at that. I suggested we skip Ronald and Thika; we could easily make Mweiga in a day. But Pru wouldn't hear of it. It will be much better for the car, she insisted. We also had to find Ansti. Having changed her plans, she was now quite cozy with me and determined to go with me to the Red Sea. Was I going to the Red Sea? Ansti seemed to have disappeared. Pru said I should be happy that I had my traveling companion back. I thought she said it rather complacently.

Among the letters we had collected, there were four from Andrew demanding with increasing urgency news of my whereabouts, my plans, my dates, whether or not I had made reservations for Christmas and so on. He claimed it was impossible for him to plan until he heard from me and why did I not answer? The last letter was quite peremptory in tone. I could understand (sort of) but not sympathize. It must have all looked quite simple to him, alone in Banagi: fix something with Ansti, or not, or in any case, make a decision, arrive at a firm plan, and inform him of it at once so he could arrange the dates of his local leave. I attributed his mind-set to having been in the army. Embedded in our immediate uncertainties, I found it irritating. The letters from the States were full of similar requests, but not as pressing. We really could not arrive at any decision without finding Ansti, and even found, we knew he might be hard to pin down. I wrote back to Andrew saying this, but from the point of view of exchanging letters time was getting short. Why didn't Andrew just set a date near Christmas for himself to come to Nairobi and tell me when he was coming? We could then work something out together. I sent a telegram, wondering if it was any use. His last letter had suggested a tented Christmas on a beach somewhere, just the two of us. He didn't know Pru was still here, of course. He said it was getting late to book a hotel. Everyone in Kenya went to the coast for Christmas. Why didn't I answer? My mother's letters demanded to know why I was not yet in South Africa seeing respectable people for a change.

On our third trip to the Avenue, we did find Elizabeth, now a much happier girl. She had, or her father had, sorted out her differences with the management. She also produced an old note for me from Ansti. How old? Elizabeth didn't know and it wasn't dated. It said I was to wire him at Thomson's Falls. "Will definitely send G back if you can give me satisfactory time." None of this mentioned Pru to her annoyance, but I pointed out that Ansti like everyone supposed she was by now on a boat with Oliver.

Just as we were discussing all this, in walked Carl, the man who had been with Ansti in the Mara. He announced that Ansti was now in the N.F.D. with Gwen. "But they'll never get through," he added. "It's all mud up there at this time of year. He's left a lot of people in Nairobi wanting to get hold of him! I'm told that if a man's jailed for personal debts he has to pay for his board at 8 A.M. every day, or he doesn't get fed. Isn't that right, Johnny?" he asked a man who'd come in with him.

As we left, they waved us off. "Where did you two crazy girls get that pensionable old bus?" they asked. We just smiled and drove off. Back at the Norfolk, we had something to eat then tried to read in the lounge. In one corner were two football enthusiasts and on the sofa and elderly man was listening patiently to a sad-looking girl with an unusually carrying voice. She seemed to be involved with an Indian, not the one she'd come out to see that her family didn't approve of and who had since *died*, but another one, his friend, who told her "Now my friend is dead, I feel I ought to look after you." She said people stared when they went out together, so now he didn't come to see her because he didn't want to embarrass her. Her voice easily over-rode the discussion of coaches and footballers of the past. "It's so very difficult," she kept saying. The old man nodded understandingly. "I've never seen a stop like that!" cried one of the footballers. "I don't believe it, man!" We went to bed.

The Thika road, a dreary road we were to travel often, was as usual under construction, obstructed by large bits of machinery and gangs of convicts. We got through the police barrier and made for the Blue Posts Hotel. Everyone stopped at the Blue Posts. We reckoned the manager would know where Ronald was and he did. Ronald, the manager said, had been "sold. Transferred. Got a new job with another owner." He gave us yet a different phone number to try and let us use his telephone, and for a miracle, Ronald answered and gave us directions. He invited us to stay, too, but we'd already lost a day so we said we'd better get to Mweiga. He then suggested we stay on the way back. "Make Thika your headquarters until you go to the coast." This was very generous of him. "Andrew wrote you, didn't he, to ask you to come to the coast with us for Christmas?" I asked. "Yes, but I couldn't possibly go. Far too much work to do."

We said he should try, unless he had other plans. No, he had no other plans, but didn't see how he could get the time off for, as he put it, "gallivanting on the coast."

Pru looked rather disappointed. I was too. It looked as though we were back to the one man two women business unless we could find someone for Pru, and Andrew B. would not be thinking about this in the middle of the Serengeti even supposing he'd got my letter.

At Nyeri we stopped at the Outspan for directions and duly arrived at the Marrians, parking Oliver's land rover as far as possible from their immaculate lawn. They were very gracious. "How would you like to dress for dinner? Short or long" Susie asked as she conducted us to a beautiful room. The stairs were dominated by her full length

Ronald

portrait. "Oh, short, I think, we said, trying to sound casual. We didn't have any "long," and everything short was pretty travel-worn. "You must tell us *all* your adventures at dinner," she said. "Would you like a bath?" We hoped this was out of politeness and said gravely that we would indeed. Susie was an American, married at eighteen to her handsome English husband. She looked barely over eighteen now. They had two small blond children and an English governess to look after them. They were lucky, she said, living right next door to the R.A.F. station. But we noticed that guns were laid on the table alongside the cutlery. The combination of the guns and the French windows opening onto the garden made us suddenly feel rather exposed to the night and whatever it contained. They said they had guards.

They also had their own plans for the next day, flying to Nanyuki (in their own plane, of course) to do something. We assured them we would be perfectly all right, amuse ourselves and so on. Nevertheless, the governess was assigned to see to our every want. Horses were to be brought for us after breakfast, and we were told that two V.I.P. guests were due to arrive in the afternoon; Susie said we must of course entertain them until she and Peter returned.

In the morning, we found bowls of dewy roses, freshly picked from the garden, on all the tables and separate silver services for tea and coffee laid out by the slow-moving houseboys; everything was beautifully polished. In the daylight we could see how nicely sited the house was, with a fine view of the hills. Susie said they'd had a lot of trouble with elephants getting into the garden until they'd dug a huge ditch called a ha-ha around everything. She said elephants didn't care for ha-has.

The horses, held by the syce, were stamping their feet. They looked very frisky. We urged the syce to precede us, as we didn't know the paths, figuring our horses would stay behind his. To my delight, I was allotted a handsome chestnut polo pony with beautiful gaits, a pleasure to ride and we went a long way. We stuck to open ground, though. One never knew.

Later, when Andrew and I went to Nyeri, I took him to the Marrians to introduce him and they made all sorts of plans to fly down to the Serengeti to visit us. They were delighted with the idea of our future life and Susie thought us both "very sweet." I thought they would find our P.W.D. bungalow rather a contrast to their own establishment, and the water supply even more so.

We left the Marrians on the 15th and drove to Ronald's new estate. His house lay beyond acres of coffee plants and down some very dark lanes ideal for ambushing a planter coming home in the dusk. Ronald's previous assistant had been attacked and badly butchered (he still lived), but there were no guards to be seen and we wondered about the danger. Ronald brushed this aside when we mentioned it, but from all we had heard it is very easy to be casual, until it's too late. In fact, at

Christmas, General Wavell's son was ambushed and killed at Thika, not far from the notorious Thika gorge near the very estate Ronald was managing. But Ronald stayed lucky.

Andrew, for his part, stayed lucky too, and not for lack of exposure to danger. When we were at last together again, he explained the reason for his frequent demands for my dates and plans: he had decided that instead of sitting through the rainy season in the Serengeti, where he could do nothing, he would, as soon as Christmas was "over." (as he put it), volunteer to the police or army and take an active role in the Emergency He planned to form a small mobile force to track and fight Mau Mau gangs in the forests of Mt. Kenya or the Aberdares, the two worst trouble spots, somewhere where, as he said, "there was something doing." He said his training fitted him for this and he thought he ought to "contribute."

I was appalled. I thought the idea completely quixotic. At university, which I had attended at the time of the Korean War, any male who could reasonably find a way not to be sent to Korea was avoiding the fight. Now here was Andrew, older, already a veteran of World War II in Burma, eager to fight against notoriously vicious thugs who were not even soldiers. The news every day was of beheadings, dismemberments and worse, usually of the gangs' own people (the Kikuyus) in sly, nighttime raids, or the murdering of planters, their wives and children and animals in the same way. I couldn't understand Andrew wanting to get involved. Weren't we engaged? Didn't he care? I suppose it was very American, or very young, but I felt, well, rejected. I thought a lot about this during our bittersweet Christmas.

As soon as we got back to Thika from Mweiga, I sent Andrew another telegram, "Come. We're at Ronald's" and telling him where that now was. Then we went to Nairobi to try again to find Ansti. I had had a letter from him, announcing his departure for Addis Ababa by toad on the 13th. "Wish you could have made this trip," the letter said, giving a mailing address in Addis. The letter added that because the jungle night stuff was "well scrambled between P and G it seems certain that my investment in your movie career will be very sour unless you do a big Red Sea job." Movie career? I had no illusions on that score, but it was reassuring that there was still a job for me in the Red Sea if I wanted it. As Carl had surmised, however, he and Gwen had made no headway in the N.F.D. and he was now back in Nairobi. He said he'd decided to sell the power wagon and arrange to ship the station wagon to Massawa in Eritrea. In Massawa, he would hire a boat, work with Gwen and then, on our arrival, work with us. He was surprised Pru was still here but didn't ask questions. So we were reinstated?

We claimed Christmas off, and he agreed. After Massawa Ansti said he might drive up the coast of the Red Sea (!) to north Africa, whence the vehicle would be shipped home. In my ignorance, I thought this might be an interesting way to get home ourselves, much to Pru's disgust. She said she could no longer understand me. He said he would write us a letter with his various proposals, which he did on the 19th. By then he and Gwen had moved to a hotel called the Normandy. Maybe even Ansti was getting sick of the Avenue.

Hotel Normandy, Nairobi, Dec. 19
Dear Wendy,
Will you agree to one of the following schemes:-

I. I motor via Somaliland, leaving early next week and send for you and P to come on a plane some Sunday Jan. 10 or later. I shall let G go shortly after.

II I go to Mombassa [sic] this Sunday (tomorrow), get equipment and station wagon on S.S. Diana, return to Nairobi and fly to Ethiopia.. I have customer for my truck here but you will have to collect check for £1000 and bring it to me on plane Jan.3, 10, or 17. G will go shortly after you arrive.

III. I wait here and we motor via Moyale leaving Jan 2 with both cars. G will be paid off before we leave. This plan causes maximum delay. We might not be diving until February. Question of P's visa for Ethiopia.

IV. You have decided not to come to Ethiopia at all. I will tell G that I shall need till April.

Please call me here. We were turned back from NFD by closed roads. I rather incline to No. II at present.

When we saw him, we also settled on "II." His next letter, which reached us after our return from the coast, was from a hotel in Massawa. He wanted us to check on whether or not the truck had yet been sold, also on a refund of the East African customs duty he had been charged for the station wagon. "I shall be happy to be with you again," he added, which I thought really nice of him after all the troubles he'd had with us—"providing," he added, "you are all set to work and live on boat for series of voyages." He asked us to get 500 electric blasting caps which he wanted to use to "bang" fishes. He added that they might be difficult to acquire and transport but that he could get none in Massawa. Let him know by telegram time of arrival. He included an air ticket for me and was arranging another one for P but she had to get her visa first.

Christmas

A telegram on the 20th from Andrew had announced his arrival that day by air from Musoma and we only just had enough warning to meet him at the airport. Ronald drove us in the estate's limousine, and the elegant car gave me the idea for a prank: I would go into the airport alone with a gun in my belt and, gesturing at the long car, reveal that I had at last decided to become Ansti's mistress and now enjoyed all manner of luxuries preparatory to joining him on the Red Sea in my white bathing suit. I thought this hilarious. It must have come straight out of a bottle of beer, maybe more than one. It didn't work because the (unloaded) gun fell out of my belt on the waiting room floor and I was too flustered to carry off the rest.

"Let Ronnie and Pru go back to Thika," Andrew said, seeing his brother anxious to go. I have to wait for Logan Hughes. We can go out to Thika in his car."

"Logan?" I asked. "You haven't asked Logan for Christmas have you?"

"Yes. To keep Pru company. You were worried about a threesome, remember?"

"But Logan has sworn eternal love for *me*! You aren't up to date. This will never work. Pru can't stand him."

"Oh. Well. You said we couldn't go to the coast by ourselves, which is what I wanted to do, and Logan was hanging around looking mournful. Anyway, he's coming. Probably get here any minute. Can't un-invite him." We went to the New Stanley Bar to wait. We had some beer. Alone at last, apart from about sixty other people, we couldn't think what to say to each other.

"So, you're here," I managed at last.

"Yes," said Andrew. We both looked at our glasses.

We weren't left alone long. Logan was soon standing over us, looking pained as usual. "I'm here," he said miserably. "As you can see (Eeyore-like)."

When he had had a beer, we duly went out to Thika in his car.

Logan Hughes

Ronald's bungalow had three bedrooms, but one was full of stores which Ronald refused to move so Ronald and Andrew and Logan slept in Ronald's room while Pru and I shared the other. The next morning both Bagnalls complained that Hughes snored so loudly that they'd got no sleep at all, and this may have added to the generally tense atmosphere. Five was no better than three and by the time twenty-four more hours had gone by, Pru and Ronald had managed to find so much in common that they made it obvious that they'd rather none of the rest of us were around. Andrew told me Ronald kept taking him aside asking if Logan had designs on Pru. I said Andrew could reassure him on that score, but I would not like him to tell Ronald about Hughes and me. Andrew had little patience with what he called Hughes' mooning. "Pay no attention," he advised me. "He's always mooning over some girl."

"But he's here," I said. "You asked him. He can't be left out all the time." Pru considered Logan none of her business. "We'd better take him into Nairobi with us when we go." We were always going into Nairobi for something.

Andrew at once became very impatient with both Hughes and me.

"Going to be a fine Christmas," he muttered. I agreed, but we had to go through with it. We hadn't even reached the coast yet.

By day two at Thika, Logan was sulking properly. Said he'd decided he wouldn't come to the coast. Wasn't wanted. He could see he wasn't wanted. Didn't know why he'd been asked. Being made a fool of. Everyone now felt sorry for him and tried to reassure him. I tried to jolly him up. I didn't want to see him hurt just because he'd been foolish enough to fall in love with me. The Pru-Ronald business was unexpected after all, so soon after Oliver. Couldn't we rustle up another female for him?

It then developed that Logan had friends on the coast and when he'd said he was coming down there with some people they'd offered him their house. Accommodation problem solved—if we could persuade him to stay with us. He had also said he knew of a boat we could rent. Everyone brightened up. We could sail up to Lamu, the old Arab town on the coast just south of Somalia. After all, we'd be four down on the coast as Ronald wasn't coming. Come on—let's go!

The person not ready to go was Andrew. He said he still had to clear his papers with the police. He had to see the dentist. He had to get a police uniform made, and a mess jacket. While he was doing all these things, Logan trailed around with me while I did Ansti's errands. He had nothing whatever to do but brood on the sadness of life. We noticed that whenever we sat down as a group for a beer or a meal, he would take out a folded piece of paper and write something on it, occasionally lifting his eyes from the paper to stare at one or another of us, then bend his head to his task again. He went on insisting that he was a burden to us. His emotions left him feeling weak, he said. Us too. He didn't leave, though, and we tried to make things as agreeable for him as we could. Nor was it dire all the time either. Every time we went to Nairobi we'd meet up with friends and end up having some kind of party with them, and Logan enjoyed all the jollity in spite of himself. The alternative, after all, was a lonely morose Christmas in Mtu wa Mbu.

The days were passing. We kept making resolves to leave and at last there was a last evening. We would celebrate by dressing nicely and going to the Travellers Club. We would change in Nairobi. Ronald would join us, already changed, from Thika. We arranged to meet at the New Stanley as usual.

Ronald arrived punctually, immaculately dressed, to find that none of us had yet changed and that we had somehow "picked up" another man we'd met at the bar and thought looked lonely. This was Mike (not the Arusha Mike, another one), who said he was waiting for his car to be delivered from Mombasa. We all, including Pru, had urged Mike to join our table, so he did. The more people the better, we reckoned.

In the New Stanley bar

Ronald, however, did not approve of picking people up and was very stiff. He kept looking at his watch and then at us until we scurried off to change. I am afraid we were all very lax and sloppy by Ronald's standards, and I imagined Pru being seriously quizzed, when they were alone, along the lines of "how have you put up with Andrew and Wendy all this time?"

To get to Mombasa, we were planning to take Oliver's and Logan Hughes' land rovers and we were packed and ready to go when we found that Oliver's land rover had, all by itself in the night, developed its old clutch trouble again. Another day's delay? No! We'd take it to the garage and drive down that night. It would be cooler then anyway. We met Mike again. He said he'd heard that his car was caught up in some kind of bureaucratic tangle. Any chance of a lift down with you? Sure, we said . No problem. We told him about the clutch. "Let's plan to meet about five and see what the situation is then."

"Fine. I'll see you then." He stood in the New Stanley doorway watching us go off down the street. He had a slightly puzzled look on his face in our company. It may have been habitual, but we supposed he found us all crazy.

We met at five with the land rover fixed, but we didn't leave. Some one of us, I don't remember who, had figured out that if we left at five we'd get to Mombasa at midnight and then what would we do? We must obviously delay our departure. We phoned Ronald and he came in to town and we all decided to go to the movies. As we couldn't agree on what to see, we tossed matches. Ronald, Pru and Logan went to one and Mike, Andrew and I to another. That is, we thought Logan had gone to the movies with Ronald and Pru, but he had not. He had left them, muttering "two's company" and disappeared.

Where? We went to where the land rovers were parked (in the hotel garage) and found that all the baggage that had been allotted to Hughes' was now dumped in it on top of our stuff. Oliver's elderly springs were flattened under the load. Still, Logan might not have decamped completely. Might he not be, even now, back at the bar awaiting our pleas for him to rejoin us? It would have been like him.

We were right. We found him sitting with someone called Simon, who had been getting an earful of all his troubles. We walked over and asked to join them. No one said anything about the land rovers. We chatted. I asked if he'd got the petrol for the trip. We even drank a toast: To Mombasa! But he was not to be jollied out of his decision. He asked me to step outside. He said, "I am not going." I feigned surprise. He said he could stand it no longer. "It will be better for everyone if I don't go" He would find something to do with himself, he added rather ominously, and walked off, leaving me standing in the street.

I rushed back in, and Andrew rushed out. He looked up and down the avenue. Ah, there he was! But Logan no sooner caught sight of Andrew than he rushed at him, waving his letter in his hands, "This is for you," he cried and turned to leave. Andrew reached out and grabbed his arm.

"See here," he said. "You know you're leaving us in the lurch, don't you?"

But he could get nothing out of him, and he was embarrassed to be seen holding another man back by force in the street. As a parting shot, he said "Come, my dear fellow—I understand about your feelings but can't you see you're leaving Pru without a companion for Christmas?" But Logan tore his arm away and made off down the block.

Andrew came back in, furious. "He's always getting these calf-sick bouts of deathless love. By next spring if not before it will be someone else, someone equally impossible for him to marry, and that love will be just as all-consuming."

Ronald then, reluctantly, offered us his own car. It was a black four-door affair, very city. We all appreciated that this must have been a difficult offer for him to make, but we accepted gratefully. Then he said, well, with Hughes pushing off he might after all join us. But he had to go back to Thika first to arrange things, join us later, perhaps on Christmas day. "On the other hand," he added, "I'm sot sure I can get away, if at all…"

This seemed to rule out taking his car. Mike stayed aloof from these skirmishes, wanting only to get to Mombasa. In the end, he helped us unload Oliver's land rover and we ruthlessly eliminated every unnecessary item, putting them in Ronald's car to be taken back to Thika. We were still hoping to get a cancellation in a hotel in Malindi. For some reason we took the spirit lamp with us just in case. This was a mistake. Kicked around on the floor of the land rover it emitted fumes of methylated spirit all the way, and was never used.

It was a ghastly trip, three in the front and one of us taking turns to sit in the back among the luggage. Mike, wishing I think to make sure we all got there, did most of the driving. By the time we arrived, we all felt rotten: the fumes, the road, no food and all that beer. We drove round and round the steaming town, helping Mike find his car. We finally deposited him at the shipyard. Andrew slept through the goodbyes. I was driving at that point. But we had to wake Andrew up at the shipyard gates because the guard decided not to let us out. He was very firm and said we must be searched. Andrew explained we had only come in a minute ago. "That does not matter, Bwana. You may have cigarettes from the boat." Andrew began to look angry. As I said, none of us were in good condition. He got out and "had a word" with the guard's superior and we drove out.

At the Mansion House, then the only decent hotel in Mombasa (full of course), we had an early lunch and began to feel better. We set out for Malindi, seventy miles north. I continued to drive for a while, but after ten miles had to give up. I was having serious stomach pains, and I felt sick, and I knew what that meant: find somewhere off the road—quick. I slid down the bank towards a small tree I'd spotted. It wasn't much, but it would have to do. I threw up the soup and the delicious salad and a few other things I didn't remember having eaten, then I had to deal with diarrhea at the other end. I was squatting as tight to the ground as I could, when a very snooty-sounding English female voice floated down from the roadside. Her car had stopped near ours. "I do hope," the voice said, "that the weather will be decent in Malindi."

I looked up and thought what I was doing must be painfully obvious from the road, but I couldn't help it. I looked down again and waited for her to push off so I could creep back to the car.

Andrew said, "If you're sick we'd better not go to Malindi."

So Mombasa would be better? I told him I'd be all right. I certainly hoped so. If only the stomach pains would stop.

After the second ferry crossing, I announced that I was sorry but I had to throw up again. I was longing not to be a nuisance. Both Andrew and Pru were very kind. Pru found a washcloth damp from the morning; Andrew held my head. They were very patient. Andrew then decided it was foolish to go on to Malindi where there was no doctor. I said I didn't need a doctor. I'd be all right. But I was overruled. We turned back. It was very discouraging for us all. I really believed that if I could only sleep for a little, I would be all right. Then I had another sharp attack of the trots. There was nowhere to hide and no less than three cars materialized on that empty road, one full of curious Indians, and on foot, a noisy group of African women with their children took their time passing. What a nightmare.

Once back in the car I stretched out on the baggage and fell so fast asleep that the return to Mombasa passed very quickly. I only woke once, to find an African peering at me curiously, so I shut my eyes again.

It was now Christmas eve, and we had no place to go; Pru had more or less collapsed too (with fatigue) by now. Andrew was wonderful. He scouted around and found a dump that would take us. Flights of dirty stairs, a hot airless room, only a bucket to wash in, but shelter. I was still feeling weak, but better. Pru was not. Suddenly she lit into me. She was so tired and discouraged, she said; nothing had gone right for her, and now here she was stuck with me and Andrew again and she just couldn't stand it and she knew I wasn't feeling well but the least I could do was stop crying.

Andrew knocked loudly on the door. "Anyone coming for some food?" He sounded very hearty. Pru said at once that she could not eat a thing and was going straight to bed. I thought I'd better go, not to eat, but to keep him company. I dried my eyes and put a brush through my hair.

On a Mombasa street

We spent Christmas day wandering around the Mombasa markets and the Arab quarter. Pru said nothing most of the time. Our hotel room was much too disagreeable to stay in during the day, so she had to put up with us. We had all given up on Malindi and when it did not look as though Ronald would turn up. Andrew took us down the coast to a small hotel he knew called the Twiga ("giraffe"). It was on a beach so at least we could have a swim. I remember thinking how beautiful he looked, coming towards me across the sand, and what a romantic Christmas we might have had in that tent he'd suggested, if only I were free of conventional restraints, if only there were just the two of us to consider, if only...

The next day, after phoning Ronald, we went back to Thika. Andrew and I found it necessary to get out of the house during the day so we went into Nairobi as usual though without the party atmosphere. One day Andrew took me to a small jewelry shop. "You ought to have a ring," he said.

"I don't need a ring," I was conscious of his low salary and his present expenses.

"Pick one out. I want you to have one."

I gazed unwillingly at the rings. Any ring that resembled an engagement ring, that is, something with a diamond no matter how small, on it, looked very expensive. In a corner, my eye was caught by a small topaz, my birthstone. "That one will do." He took me at my word, went in and bought it. "Put it on." I did, but felt so self-conscious that I soon took it off again before we went back to Thika. I didn't want there to be any discussion of rings.

All too soon, Andrew's papers and clothes were ready and he was depressingly eager to "be off" to report to the police station in Fort Hall. I drove him there in Oliver's land rover. We called on the Marrians and then it was goodbye, in public, at the police station. He got out of the car and went into the office, taking his kit. In a few minutes he was back. "They've just captured a Mau Mau 'general.' Want to have a look?" He led me to the police cells. In one of them an African man was sitting on his heels. He did not appear to be injured physically. I looked at his face briefly, feeling embarrassed and he glared back. I wished I had said no. We went back to the car.

"There's a sergeant that wants a lift back to Thika. He'll go with you. Good idea on that road."

"All right."

"Well, goodbye then."

"Goodbye. Be careful." He nodded and turned away. I knew it not the place to exchange fond kisses, but I was sorry. I wondered if I really would see him again.

The sergeant, a large man, got placidly into the passenger seat and we drove off. I dropped him at the Blue Posts as he asked.

Prudence Has Her Turn

Ah, now, Pru had all the revenge for being with Andrew and me that she could wish for! After several days, she informed me that she and Ronald were really in love. Their courting consisted of spending lots of time playing Ronald's classical records and then in musical discussions focused on detailed analyses. "Such a delightful little coda," they agreed as the well-worn seventh was played again. No one was allowed to talk during the music of course, not that I wanted to. My only relief was describing all this in my diary. The diary was a great comfort.

After a week a letter came from Andrew describing his askaris and trackers. He seemed to be on his own with them most of the time, camping in the forest and trying to ambush the gangs on their way to or from their attacks. He was enjoyed the challenge, had a good bunch of people, and so on. There was nothing personal in the letters. The occasional gunfights were well described. I hated reading about the gunfights. Stuck in Thika, quite near him geographically and yet very far away mentally, nothing seemed more desirable to me now than to get to the Red Sea. I could understand how little the appeal of going back to Ansti had for Pru, but we had both agreed to Plan II, and she knew Ansti would never pay her fare home if she didn't show up. The planes for Ethiopia left once a week. When we got Pru's visa and I suggested we ought to be leaving. Pru said there was no hurry. Ansti still had Gwen. Leaving now was quite unnecessary. She said it was very selfish of me, considering all she'd had to put up with in the Serengeti and Mombasa.

I wrote a lot of letters home, trying to catch my mother up, and in my diary described how irritating I found Ronald, and Pru when in his company. She was behaving quite differently from the girl I'd been traveling with. With Ronald she was very serious. Indeed they never seemed to laugh at anything. I couldn't help wondering about what it would be like having them as sister and brother-in-law and found no pleasure in it.

Fortunately, Ansti kept sending telegrams asking for our date of arrival. They got shorter and shorter. The last one just said "Advise." Then, in a letter written on January 9th, he told us to get visas for the Sudan. A letter on the 11th from Port Sudan explained that he'd given up on Eritrea because he could not get a boat. I figured we still had to travel via Ethiopia because those were the only tickets we had; and besides it would be interesting.

During the hours Ronald was busy on the coffee estate, we did all Ansti's errands, enquired about the truck, still unsold, and the station wagon, still unshipped. Would he want it shipped now that he was no longer in Massawa? We telegraphed for instructions. Yes, he did, but to Port Sudan and when were we coming? He was keeping Gwen until we arrived (extra expense). He sent me some money, but was not going to pay hotel time or traveling time until we were with him. Pru thought this "the meanest thing" she'd ever heard, but I was inclined to be sympathetic. He had sent me a copy of a letter to his advisers in Boston about his finances. He was trying to juggle the costs of filming, so far unsuccessfully, and of three assistants, and the worries this gave him probably accounted for a lot of the way he behaved. But Pru didn't care to make allowances. The shared pay of five dollars a day was already very low and she said he should certainly pay all our expenses. Ronald of course agreed, and they both blamed me for being unbusinesslike.

Red Sea Hotel, Port Sudan, Jan.15th COPY TO W.
(To his financial advisers):

"I am writing Mrs. Owen at length about my financial difficulties...

"During my seven months in East Africa I spent $10,000 but actually only $7000 went into operations. The three thousand additional was the cost of bringing out an extra assistant from Hollywood and then returning her there, when my original two young ladies emerged from the Tanganyika bush, and rejoined the expedition. I really operated on $1000 a month as estimated, but am doubtful as to the value of this film.

"I am now preparing to work for three or four months under the Red Sea in hopes of finishing up my [underwater] film. I face an unexpected [sic] exspence [sic] in having to replace all my old diving equipment by the modern aqualung. These were used by Dr. Hans Hass in his successful; picture "Under the Red Sea," which is much better than anything I have…[it] will make competition very tough. Of course I have always built my films around record dives [i.e. in the bathysphere]. I had planned to bring the current opus out with a mile dive off California next summer. In this field I am now completely knocked out of the box by Prof. Picard (69) two miles down.

"I feel, therefore, that my prospects as an explorer have been darkened and that I shall have to look for something else to do, trying to take comfort in the fact that it took two very unusual men to bring me down.

"It seems to me that it is best to operate here until June and try to bring my film to the point where it may be sold - even at a loss, unless you advise a fold up at once."

In another letter (to me) written at about the same time, he said that the "Red Sea Fisheries Officer" had invited us all "to stay on an island 120 [miles] to the north [of Port Sudan] where he has a station. He will lend us some small boats, but we shall have to live ashore. No big boats are available. I shall have to send to London for a compressor—such are the delays."

"P.S. [After more advice about the visas for the Sudan] "I am relying on the station wagon to get us home…I suppose we shall have to operate until some time in May to make up for lost time. Please check…about the power wagon…"

Meanwhile my mother was gradually getting used to the idea of an "African" son-in-law, African in the sense that that is where he proposed to live with her only child. During my enforced idleness n January, I told her more about Andrew and relayed what little information I had about his family, and by this time he also had written her. I later found out that she had immediately "investigated" him through her friends in the British consulate in New York and that he appeared to be all right: good war record/no criminal record—that sort of thing. I remember feeling very insulted when I heard about this, but, after all, was it so unreasonable? Now she seemed to be settling down relatively happily planning a big wedding on Cape Cod the following September (1954), to which Andrew had a bit reluctantly agreed. Her letters asked for lists of the friends I wanted to invite, lists of his friends, lists of her friends, and asked about the kind of food I wanted and so on, and what did I want in the way of wedding presents? I began to feel the same way as Andrew about all this planning and the size of it all, and the number of total strangers he would have to meet, and be inspected by. The whole production seemed to be snowballing and the contrast to the simplicities of our future life in the middle of the Serengeti was very marked.

Then Andrew himself introduced another variable. He wrote that although being a game ranger was a nice life and fine for a bachelor, he thought it would be more sensible to get a farm in East Africa, a rented one if it were in Tanganyika. At thirty-one it was time, he said, that he "settle down and raise a family." I was still twenty-one with a lot more "exploring" to do and I'm afraid by first reaction was dismay. A farm? A sedentary life? Children? What did I want with children? It was all very pleasant the way the Marrians did it, but I knew we would never have that kind of money. I had no constructive alternative suggestion to make but I was sure I didn't want to farm or to have children any time soon.

I suppose I also couldn't help but absorb the idea that the era of the white colonial settler was coming to an end. Everyone talked of it. In the 1920s young Englishmen had been encouraged to settle in Kenya to develop the colony and its agriculture. My own English cousin had wanted to do so just after World War I. It was then regarded as a wonderful opportunity. But now the Mau Mau emergency was only the most visible evidence of the way "things" might and probably would go: towards "Africa for the Africans," towards independence (*uhuru*). The spirit of the times was anti-colonial, particularly in America. The British in Kenya talked resentfully about this too: how the Americans simply did not understand how a fair administration and reasonable infrastructure had improved the lives of the native, and how we were in a hurry to throw all that good work away. Who were the Americans to talk? Look at their blacks! Look at the American Indians! Contrast how these people have been treated with our selfless colonial administration. They were often very angry and being Americans we were in the firing line.

Andrew's idea of a farm, therefore, would not have been a good plan for the future for all sorts of reasons most of which were just over the horizon and I cannot claim to have foreseen them. All I knew was that I wasn't ready to "settle down." Yes, I thought Andrew just the right sort of person, but what I loved about his life was its freedom.

Ronald had quite a lot to say on this subject. He said that people who'd been in the war in Burma were often like Andrew, loners evading responsibilities and living in the wilds. He made living in the wilds sound just as reprehensible as evading responsibilities. He said I had my head in the clouds, and Pru, with my "soft" attitude to Ansti in mind, agreed. After racketing around with the unreliable Ansti, Pru evidently found Ronald's conventional views comforting. Her feet were on the ground all right. But the combination of the farm idea and all those wedding plans was beginning to make me feel trapped.

It must have been about this time that by mistake I left my diary in the living room when Pru and I went off to do errands in Nairobi. When we came back, it soon came out that Ronald had read it, and furthermore he had shown it to Pru and she had read it too. There was a fearful row. They were hurt and angry and very offended, and I was angry and offended too. How could anyone have the gall to read a private diary? There was no answer to that. Ronald said he was "sorry," but then kept going on at me about what a petty vindictive person I was and how I didn't understand Pru, and while he was at it, how Andrew never took the trouble to understand all his (Ronald's) problems, and how if Andrew were even a little sensitive, he would see how he was always hurting him, and how he knew Andrew thought him inferior, and so on. Then, not looking the least sorry, he reviewed all the mean things I'd said all over again. I wrote Andrew and told him, furiously, what I thought of his brother.

Ethiopia

By the time Andrew got the letter we were already in Ethiopia.

We left Nairobi very early in the morning, as we had arrived seven months ago. It felt like a round trip, a closure. We flew low over Mt. Kenya, about 500 feet above the peak; we saw a seedy-looking glacier and several small lakes with ice or scum on them, we couldn't tell which. The Mau Mau still infested Mt. Kenya's thickly forested lower slopes. Perhaps we were flying over Andrew. North of Mt. Kenya, in spite of the rains, Africa looked just as dry as when we first arrived: miles and miles of yellow-brown desert with the expanse of Lake Rudolf, also brown, glinting in the sunlight as we neared the Ethiopian border Once in Ethiopia, the land below became mountainous and even more barren.. The Swedish captain's voice came on over the intercom. "We have lots of time and lots of fuel and it's a beautiful day, so we will go to look at Bushafto, the crater lake south of Addis. You can see the Emperor's private landing field just below us now," but no one saw much through the clouds. After this we were kept busy with a customs form and its mysterious boxes labeled "Manifest No. and "Way No." and, on landing, we spent a long time battling with a lot of clerical obstruction over our cameras, especially my cine camera, and the blast caps. Everything had to be written down in Amharic, whose letters resembled runes and was written very slowly. The customs officials insisted on keeping our passports too, in spite of our protests. The Ethiopians impressed us as a difficult, nervy, arrogant people and I missed the easy-going East Africans.

Finally we made our way to the Ras Hotel. We had been told "everybody" stayed at the Ras. I spent the trip in from the airport talking with a Filipino commercial traveler who thought Cape Town a very good place, but did not think the selection of cinemas in Nairobi wide enough to make a week's stay completely enjoyable.

Addis appeared a drab sort of place compared to Nairobi, though perhaps it was just the time of year. It is very high (8000 feet) and dry and the hotel was sited inconveniently at the bottom of a long steep hill, the town center being at the top. On the way down we saw lots of empty building sites surrounded by quite elaborate walls and closed gates. We asked why the walls were built first and we told it was "to stop animals dropping stool." An enormous ceremonial arch spanned the main street, its feet still resting in piles of rubble.

The Ras was gloomy and cold and peculiar in layout. The dining room, for example, was two floors up, on the same floor as our bedroom. The "ex-pats" staying at the hotel, however, were very friendly, particularly the Americans working for Point IV, and at once wanted to show us the sights. So did an Egyptian man, Mr. Youssif, who claimed he knew more and cornered us into accepting.

He drove fast and badly but was very thorough. Sight number one was the Emperor's lion. The Emperor always kept a lion, Lion of Judah being one of his titles, but it was a pathetic mangy beast. What a contrast to the Banagi lions. The Milottes would have hated to see it pacing its bare cage, eking out its miserable existence, and so did we. We were then shown a large ornate structure the Italians had intended as an Opera House but never got the chance to use. As there were only three hundred or so Europeans then living in Addis, there was little hope for such a project now. The Emperor had given the building to the Duke of Harar, one of his sons, who had installed in it a "Photolite Studio," a machinery supply place, and the "Imperial Shoa Dairy"— distribution only, we guessed as we saw no cows. It was apparently a habit of the Emperor to bestow various structures on his family. The Empress was to have a new apartment building, under construction, as of 1954, for three years and not even half-finished. Meanwhile, she enjoyed the ownership of, and considerable revenue from, the capital's *tedj* houses. *Tedj*, a kind of mead, is the national drink. *Tedj* houses generally doubled as houses of ill-repute, we were told with a wink, so the Empress had become very rich. Mr. Youssif said he was very fond of *tedj*, as of all drink, he added. He was kind enough to take us to a bank to change some money, which took a long time, and entertained us with stories from the time he had "been with" the British army in North Africa. Good drinking times, we gathered.

In the afternoon, we went by ourselves to a soccer game. We thought it was going to be a horse race until a lot of men in colored shorts ran out onto the field. It proved to be a match between the Ethiopians and the Yugoslavs and they played for what seemed a very long time before there was a break. Outside the barriers, a lot of men in dirty jodhpurs kept carrying stones from one pile to another so as to see the game without having to pay. There were several such piles and people kept falling off them amid raucous laughter. In the break there was a bicycle race. We were told the Emperor was in attendance and hoped for a glimpse, but he stayed hidden behind his flowered screens. The Yugoslavs won, but suffered a lot of injuries.

That evening we were introduced to the cuisine of the Ras hotel and understood why other things to see and do in Addis consisted mostly of going somewhere else to eat.

There were many little Italian-looking restaurants that gave us hope, pretty places hung with vines, with views out over the hills, but the Chianti was very rough and the food a travesty of Italian food, the pasta locally made and very tough and the sauces seriously hot. The alternative was Ethiopian food, consisting of even hotter sauces, served on *njera*, circular platters of unleavened bread. Raw meat cut fresh from the cow, mentioned in nearly all the travel books, was not in evidence.

Everything accomplished by the Italians was much admired by the foreigners working in Ethiopia. The general opinion was that "the Brits" ought to have left them to it. In six years the Italians had built all the better buildings and all the roads, their most famous and most appreciated being the road between Addis and Asmara, a miracle of engineering and sound construction. There was nothing like it. True, the Italian prisoners of war had built the road descending the rift valley escarpment from the Ngong hills in Kenya, but this was a far longer and more difficult feat, with several hundred miles of broken country with sheer-sided hills, deep valleys, and seasonally turbulent rivers to cross. We, Pru and I, should not even think of flying between Addis and Asmara if we could go by road, said the Austrian manager of the Ras Hotel, who just then joined our group. "In two days you could go in my car!" he cried enthusiastically. "I have to send the car and driver to Asmara in two days. There you are! You can go with him."

It was quickly settled and we got a lift back up the hill to try to talk the Ethiopian Airlines clerk into changing our Addis-Asmara tickets into Asmara-Port Sudan. He was most unwilling to do this and much distracted by an elderly joker who kept snatching the rubber stamps from his desk and stamping everything within reach while the clerk tried to hold him off. It took two hours of sitting in his small office before he finally consented.

Conflicting programs were arranged for our entertainment the next day. The assistant manager, also an Austrian, invited us to go riding with him, and Larry (Point IV) insisted on driving us to Lake Bushafto. Larry was writing an Ethiopian Geography for Ethiopians. Through a misapprehension we found the manager had given the assistant manager the next day off also specifically to take us to Bushafto, so we explained and asked him to give his assistant the following day off instead, which he did. The manager was just as determined as his clientele to ensure that his guests saw and did everything. After the build-up, Bushafto proved disappointing: swarms of flies and Swedes (the senior staff of Ethiopian Airlines were all Swedish at that time.) But the countryside was beautiful and we were told about many other crater lakes which we never saw.

We did not, however, go riding. The assistant manager, when we knocked on his door, called to us weakly from his bedroom and told us he had an attack of malaria. He begged us to sit with him and talked to us steadily for a long time, in spite of his fever, and showed us his entire collection of photographs. After lunch Pru said she wasn't feeling well, so I went to get our passports out of the customs, and then to the immigration office to extend our temporary visas for long enough to reach and then leave Asmara.

There is camaraderie, I found, among people waiting in immigration offices. You may come from different countries but you all have the same problem: persuading the clerk in front of you to adjust what is already stamped into your passport by some other clerk, and this on his own initiative. I soon made friends with a Japanese gentleman who said he was in Africa to open the market for Japanese textiles even though his university degree was in engineering. When his passport was finished and all the details had been recorded in triplicate, he took a formal farewell of me, bowing, shaking my hand and telling me to take care of myself and to see that no harm became me, and thanked me for our acquaintanceship. On my side, I expressed much concern for his health and wished him prosperity in business on this continent and for the years to come. We shook hands again, he bowed and we parted. It was quite sad.

I resumed my argument with the immigration clerk. In the end I only got our visas extended by seeing the head of the department, a Mr. Alfred, who was very severe with me but eventually wrote a long letter in Amharic for me to show three other people and the clerk. The clerk then reminded me that it was the custom here to pay $10.00. He didn't seem to mind when I signed Pru's name for her, and we parted on good terms.

On The Road to Asmara

The car and its chauffeur, a small thin man named Gasfar, were ready early and we settled into the back seat for our long ride. I would have liked to study a map as we went but it would have made me carsick because of the many switchbacks and hairpin curves. Books on Ethiopia describe the terrain as cut with a knife, and before the Italian road it took many days to travel between Addis and the coast, descending perilously into the ravines on rough tracks, fording almost impassable rivers and then climbing laboriously up the cliffs on the far side. There were many places we would have liked to photograph, particularly some of the dramatic descents. In one place even Italian engineering had given out; a bridge was down and our elegant car, a dark blue Mercedes, had to ford a stream over its hubcaps in boisterous water.

On the road to Asmara

It took us all day to reach a place called Dessie ("Dess-i-eh")

153

where we stopped for the night. All afternoon we tried to maintain a lively interest in the scenery of small huts on the edges of ravines and the occasional horseman, wrapped in a shawl and wearing the local jodhpurs, trotting along the roadside, but eventually I went to sleep. Pru claimed she was never able to sleep in a car, but my problem was keeping awake. Either way the hours passed slowly and when we finally stopped outside a low unadorned building with "Hotel" on a signboard over it was late and we were exhausted. The driver must have been tired too but perhaps he was used to it. We were given a small dark room immediately beside the eating room. It had a basin so I tried to turn on the tap. Nothing, not even a trickle. A spider sat in the bowl, watching me. With a big effort I made the tap squeak slightly and the spider edged toward the drain which made me think that at some time during the spider's life there had once been water. The toilet was down a long dark passage and the paper provided was, I noted with interest, pieces of the Wall Street Journal threaded on a string. It was very cold, or perhaps we were just tired and hungry. Pru pulled back the cover on her bed and something flew out. At least it flew. It was getting very dark. A man knocked on the door and without waiting entered the room to give us a stub of candle. We noticed there was no lock on the door. There was no lock on the door of the communal bathroom either and when I went to wash, I walked in on our chauffeur shaving.

Being fresh from the British sphere of influence, we decided some hot tea would be nice, so we went to sit where there were chairs, in the entrance way. A single bulb hung from the ceiling, shedding a little soft light on the figure of the manageress as she strode back and forth and, in one corner, on some men playing cards. A faint clatter off stage gave us hope of something to eat. We got our tea, in a glass as was the custom, and drank it, like two little English ladies, huddled in our own corner. Goodness knows what sort of card game it was. Players kept getting up, leaving their cards face down on the table, then someone else would come along and pick them up.

Suddenly the outside door burst open and the room filled with Italians, short fat Italians, older and younger, all similar in girth. The youngest and least fat wore very abbreviated shorts and smiled incessantly, revealing a mouthful of bad teeth. Food (see a previous description) was then put on a table and everyone gathered around and helped themselves.

We went to bed in our clothes because of where our room was and because we were so cold.

The road was even more tortuous and the scenery more beautiful the next day though after East Africa the infrequent birds were disappointingly drab, mostly large crows flying from crag to crag. We never saw another car. We passed women herding donkeys piled high with hides and others tending large horned cattle, and once we drove right up to a fine horse in a bridle with a wooden bit. It stood in the middle of the road and did not wish to move. Every other thing or person except that horse was unceremoniously given a blast of Gasfar's horn and then covered in our dust as we passed.

We spent our second night at Adigrat after fourteen and a half hours on the road. Dessie, we found in retrospect, was a "big" place compared to Adigrat. With much shouting, directions to the back of the hotel were obtained so the Mercedes could be safely stabled in its courtyard for the night. We could see why. As soon as we stopped, we were surrounded by a rowdy crowd all shouting things we thought we were fortunate not to understand, and a policeman turned up to establish order by cuffing those he could reach and sending them into what we mistook for a cellar but turned out to be the hotel entrance, very dark and unlit. We were given a room and a piece of candle and told we had to eat in the room because, the chauffeur explained, he was fearful for our bags should we leave them. We did not object. We could see, every time the door was opened, that the rest of the hotel was a bar. After some food, he continued to watch over us, popping in frequently while we were trying to undress to make sure we were all right. He asked us where we would eat breakfast, but this turned out to be unnecessary as we were never offered any. As on the day before, he came to our door at five thirty in the morning, calling out "It is over" and we were on the road again by six.

Espresso bar, Eritrea

155

From Adigrat's nearly 11.000 foot altitude we climbed down through mesa plateau country, the bare earth sides of these flat-topped hills showing clear strata of differently colored deposits, austere but beautiful. There were stone houses and the ruins of stone houses everywhere but few people. To our surprise we stopped for breakfast at one of these stone houses; inside there was a gleaming espresso machine and neat ladies in gowns with puffed sleeves served us. We were now in Eritrea. The scenery resembled a series of stage backdrops placed one in front of the other: a set of cliffs in the foreground, a deep cleft (invisible) then more hills, and snaking up and over and down and through the scenes the Italian road flowed, beautifully guttered in cement. In the middle of nowhere, a small bent man armed with a spade appeared to clear away some fallen rocks. He was quickly removed by Gasfar leaning on the horn and we passed him in a swirl of dust. I saw him shake his turbaned head. Just after Adi Caie we reached the top of a long climb to see before us a vast abyss filled with haze: the coastal plain. "Pity it isn't the sea," Pru said as the road twisted down into the haze then straightened out and made for Asmara.

The chauffeur dropped us at the Ciao Hotel where we had made a booking after smiling at us and wishing us well. Politely he did not look at what we hoped was an adequate present, just disappeared in the dust covered car.

Asmara proved far more to our taste than Addis. Warmer, more attractive and much more lively, part of the liveliness being provided by a large American army base. As we emerged from under the hotel portico, we were astonished to see, at the end of the street, *Gwen* , arm in arm with two American servicemen and looking very beautiful and of course very sexy. "Gwen!" we cried, and rushed towards her, and she seemed equally pleased to see us. "I have a story to tell you two," she said. "Have I got a *story*! What are you doing tonight?" She turned to her escorts. "We'll get some guys for these girls and we'll go paint the town, shall we?" They nodded happily. "I'll call you later," she said over her shoulder. "Great to see you! Wait till you hear!"

Pru looked disapproving. "I'm not going out with somebody Gwen's picked up. I don't see what these men see in her anyway."

I stared at her. Was she blind? "I think it would be fun," I said. "What else are we going to do? Go to bed early again?"

"Yes," said Pru, that's exactly what I'm going to do. I'm tired, I think I've caught a cold, and I'm going to bed."

That was pretty final. We had some supper then Pru went straight upstairs, took off her clothes and got into bed. When Gwen called she said she hadn't been able to find us dates yet but she rang off before I could tell her Pru wouldn't go out anyway. It was only seven so I stayed dressed in case she called again, but on reflection I decided I shouldn't go out "on the town" on some blind date without Pru. We'd been doing most things together for seven months so it just didn't seem right. But it was depressing. I hadn't even got a good book. When it got to be nine o'clock and Gwen still hadn't phoned, I went to bed myself. I was longing to hear her story. I was longing to go out and do something—anything—except go to bed. I brooded on those long days in Thika when I had made myself scarce every evening so Pru and Ronald could be alone together, and I was sick of it. She now seemed to be immured in a "writing to Ronald-hearing from Ronald" mode and nothing else was of interest: Gwen had told her there was a letter waiting in Port Sudan for her with a Kenya postmark on it.

I, on the other hand, knowing how rarely I was likely to hear from Andrew and how occupied he was, wanted some distracting amusement to pass the time. People were always interesting. Just going out with them, providing it wasn't solo, didn't commit you to anything. I wanted to do everything and see everything I could on this trip if at the end of it I would be "settling down." Pru said I was frivolous and deeply unserious. I thought she was being too boring for words. This was not a good recipe for getting along.

We did all our errands the next day: the flight bookings, a telegram to Ansti, the visas for the Sudan. The Sudanese consul showed us photographs he'd taken of what he called "Sudanese personalities" and, for some reason, of the voting procedure in the Sudan. Females could only vote if they can prove secondary education, but presumably because there was no such requirement for males, all the ballots had little pictures of the candidates and a color, or when they run out colors, a symbol such as a hand or a spade for each. The Consul said it worked very well "in the South." I gathered he was referring to the southern Sudan with its population of illiterate Dinka and Nuer. He was of course a northerner, as were all government officials.

Gwen turned up and told us her big news: she was returning to

Nairobi and was going to marry Steve. Steve certainly seemed the nicer of the two men we'd seen her with the day before; the other one, Bob, was too smooth. Steve came from California and I thought it might work out well. He was very kind to us, too, though he didn't have to be, helping us find places and showing us a bit of Asmara. We all had lunch together at the Oasis, an American canteen, and then went to a baseball game on the base. Baseball in Asmara was no more interesting, to me, than it was in the States, but we sat through the game chatting with Gwen and Steve. Laughing, Gwen told us how Ansti behaved in the hotel whenever they ate there: "he'd sit right behind us, glaring."

Gwen had been to a fortune teller in Port Sudan who corroborated all her plans. She told us there was a wonderful crowd of people in Port Sudan, but that Ansti probably wouldn't let us stay there for more than two days, and then we'd go to some fantastic place with a fantastic man, very nice, by the name of Veevers-Carter. "He puts on an opera cape in the evenings," Gwen added, and he's doing research on an island. He had offered the island to Ansti as a base. When he wasn't on the island he lived in an old rest house in a "dead city" somewhere south of Port Sudan. Gwen added that Ansti had been "like an iceberg" to her for the last few days she was there, which she said had been absolutely fine with her.

Our plane, an elderly Dakota, flew along the Red Sea coast and from the air the coral reefs showed up as large purple shadows in the clear water. I couldn't wait for the "big job" to begin. At Port Sudan airport, we had the usual trouble with my camera and the usual arguments but this time the camera was firmly confiscated and I felt very aggrieved. Would we be in Port Sudan long enough to get it back? Ansti had proposed to me that if I bought extra 16mm. color film and took pictures he could use that I would share in his profits. I think it was something like 2% of gross. I didn't regard this as much of an offer, considering the last seven months, but it just might be that Ansti had more expertise filming sharks and rays underwater than he had shown trying to net lions.

On the Red Sea Coast

After Asmara, the heat of midday in Port Sudan hit us like a wall. There was no shade anywhere around the bleak airport and none on the run into the town and none around the hotel either. The entrance doors stood wide open to catch what little sea breeze there was. In the harbor some freighters could be seen in the far distance. When we went to the desk to sign in, I could feel a lot of frank stares sizing us up. We had arrived just at lunchtime, in the middle of pre-lunch drinking time which we were to discover lasted from around noon to two if you wanted food, or three if by then you were too full of liquid to care. Quite a few people, nearly all male and dressed in white shirts and shorts and white knee socks, the daytime "Red Sea kit," were occupying the big low chairs where the lobby shaded into the lounge and the lounge into the bar in the open-plan ground floor. To the right of the desk there was a flight of stairs, and under the stairs I caught sight of Ansti's big diving helmet resting on its metal shoulders, just as it had at home. No Ansti, though, but no doubt he would show up. Self-consciously we went up the stairs to our room to wash, then down again to the dining room running the gauntlet of unabashed interest each time. Not having been models, like Gwen, it made us feel shy. We decided to hide in our room for the afternoon. It had a ceiling fan which moved the air around in a welcome manner.

That evening we braved the lounge for a beer. We were not to be deprived of beer by being stared at, and it tasted remarkably good even though it was no longer Tusker. Halfway down our glasses, one of these white-clad figures walked smartly up to our table, clicked his heels together, bowed, and announced that he was Mark Veevers-Carter. So this was our new "lord and master," apart from Ansti of course. He had a dark Van Dyke beard and moustache and very twinkly eyes and laughed a lot. He was, he said right away, in charge of our expedition and responsible to the Government of the Sudan to see we came to no harm; some of Ansti's wilder ideas for marine adventure had already circulated.

We told him we'd seen Gwen in Asmara. "Gwen! Really? And how is she? She was deported from here, you know."

"Deported? Whatever for?"

"For indiscrete behavior with various Sudanese gentlemen, I

understand," said Veevers-Carter gravely but still with a twinkle. "White women do not date Sudanese men in Port Sudan. It is simply *not done*. She was told to leave."

I thought this sounded pretty stuffy but typically British. "So, Gwen outraged the local mores, did she," I commented. "We'd better be careful! She's happy now," I added— "going to marry a fine young American, younger than she is, and go back to live happily ever after in California. Or so we hope."

Veevers-Carter laughed. "I'd better introduce you to a few of these people around here," he said." Gwen was here for a month, you know, but they've mostly recovered. They've all been waiting for you two to arrive. Wanting to know what happens next. Bring your beers, come into the bar, and we'll have a little session."

We learned that a "session" is a good long period of drinking preceding (or not) lunch or, in this case, dinner. Each man in turn pays for a round of drinks for everyone, and the pace of drinking is quite fast. We were not allowed to "call a round," and did not try as by then we knew this was also "not done." Nor did we attempt to match their consumption. In short order we had all the men in the bar clustered around, some of them bachelors, some of them with wives "at home:" Sidney, Sam, a couple of Ians, Frank, George, Richard. One of the Ians ran the local branch of Barclay's Bank. Most of the rest were civil servants administering various government departments. Sam said he'd "really fallen" for Gwen. He claimed he was a wounded man and might never recover. Gwen had affected them all in various ways, which was not surprising. She had even affected the beautiful Patricia, easily her equal in terms of looks, who drifted into the hotel that evening. It had been Patricia who had suggested to Gwen that they go to the fortune teller, but while Gwen came out happily, Patricia had been devastated: she was told that her husband would soon divorce her and that she would be dangerously sick, all with details so convincing to her that she took to her bed for three days. Sam, who was also devoted to Patricia, had been very sympathetic but could do nothing to comfort her. "The trouble with Patricia," he said, "is that she's a damned faithful wife. What can you say to a woman like that?"

It was unfortunate that in the middle of this discussion (and all these men) we caught sight of Ansti at the reception desk, and he of us. Unfortunate, that is, for making a new start. Ansti looked the very antithesis of the white clothed crowd, his grey shorts and shirt as usual stained with grease and his socks around his ankles. I sighed. Did he have to look so disreputable?

"You here already?" he asked as we approached. "Thought you were coming tomorrow."

"We sent you a telegram," said Pru reprovingly.

"Yeah. It said February 3rd."

"That's today."

"Well, you're here. We can get going. I'll see when this fisheries man wants to go. He'll take us in his Bedford truck."

We didn't ask where. We knew about the island from Gwen and Mark had told us its name (Umsharifa) and that it was about 120 miles up the coast. "I hope I can get my cine camera out of the customs before we go," I said.

"Blasting caps," said Ansti. "Did you get them? What about the power wagon? Bring me a check?" We filled him in on the vehicles and the blasting caps but decided it would be better to say nothing about having seen Gwen. If Gwen had got into trouble, so no doubt had Ansti.

Ansti was disappointed not to get his check and rubbed the space on his head where his hair had once been. He looked worried and older too, saddened if not wiser. But he had plans. This Veevers-Carter was going to catch him a manta ray the way he had for Hans Hass and we in our white bathing suits were to be photographed clasped in whatever those things were on either side of the ray's wide mouth. "They only eat plankton," Ansti added encouragingly. So that was all right. There was also some business to do with sharks, but he didn't go into details. I really hoped things would work out for him this time.

"How is your cine camera?" I asked, thinking of all the times it had broken down or sent its film spooling out onto the ground.

"Working," he answered shortly. Then he got that sly look on his face we knew so well. "By the way, in the interests of a united front I have set up an expedition table," he announced. Members of the expedition will eat together." We groaned to ourselves, but nodded politely. We were sure we could get out of this one.

Departure was set for the day after tomorrow so I hitched a ride with someone out to the airport to get my camera back. The customs people were quite agreeable about it, but I never did find out why they'd confiscated it in the first place. Don't ask, I thought to myself, just go by results. In the evening, we were invited by Mark and Sidney and Sam to "have dinner on the pavement." We gathered that this was what people did in Port Sudan as an alternative to the hotel's offerings. They were even tactful enough to include Ansti so the matter of the Expedition Table was temporarily shelved. Dinner on the pavement was eaten at tables outside a local Greek establishment and consisted of one dish, a tough "steak" topped by a fried egg, and all these men thought it was great value compared to the hotel. After Ethiopia it tasted good to us too. We were all very jolly and Ansti aside from his table manners behaved with restraint. Mark Veevers-Carter kept up a steady flow of amusing anecdotes and, as far as I could judge, actually got on well with Ansti. The barometer looked "set fair."

The next day Mark took us all down to Suakin. He said that as he was moving to the island he had to pack up. He had been living, as Gwen had told us, in the government rest house, a former palace, whose wide entrance was on a street of equally old buildings and whose rear overlooked the harbor. The small balconies of the two rooms Mark had been living in actually projected over the water, and we could see fish swimming among the coral heads directly below. Coral growth, exuberant in the tide-less Red Sea had finally closed Suakin as a navigable harbor and it had been abandoned in favor of Port Sudan.

Mark

While Mark packed, Ansti and Pru settled down to read some of his old magazines, but I wandered around the rest house. It was a lovely old building with big rooms and high ceilings and was surprisingly cool. The ground floor was reached by a wide and rather handsome staircase. There was a desk in one of the otherwise empty rooms and I opened the drawer. Inside was a ledger containing a long list of names, many of them Irish, of men who had either died or been invalided home while building the railway into the interior. The track crossed the desert due west to Atbara on the Nile, then followed the river south to Khartoum, and the cause of sickness or death was mostly, the ledger noted, heat stroke. There were a few old photographs in another room showing these "navvies" in their buttoned up shirts, woolen vests and bowler hats digging away in the hot sand under the hot sun. Mark told me later they'd also been required to wear woolen spine pads, a favorite Victorian device to absorb the sweat running down a man's back and so prevent "chills."

Outside the rest house the street was deserted except for a few cats. Mark said he used to wander around Suakin at night, semi-invisible in his opera cloak (so that's what it was for) and silent in his "tackies" – sneakers such as Andrew wore in the bush.

I could see that Mark Veevers-Carter had set himself up rather well, at least in the room he used as a living room. There were two or three nice looking Arab chests along the walls and in the center a long low table covered with a red cloth. On a box at one end of the table was a porcelain statue of Kwan Yin, the goddess of mercy, and hanging from nails on the wall a well polished naval sword his father had given him. There were candles on the table and a handsome bowl that should have held fruit, if there were any fruit to be had. All this spoke of a man much more conscious of his surroundings, interior surroundings, than Andrew Bagnall whose interests were all exterior, except maybe for painting the *choo* and putting some other color on the Banagi walls than the standard P.W.D. "buff" or "eau de nil." The bungalow at Banagi had been built and furnished by the P.W.D. so everything was rectangular and utilitarian. I had not questioned this at the time. Was there a choice? But the home Mark had made for himself in the lovely old building was completely different.

The next day, under Mark's guidance, we went to Port Sudan's *suk* to get food supplies. In this department also, Mark's ideas were much more eclectic that Andrew's or even Oliver's. He had been in Malaysia after the war and liked all rice-based dishes, with plenty of spices. I thought Ansti would not care for such a diet and would start complaining about his ulcer again, but we decided he'd have to manage. Potatoes and European vegetables could hardly be found, and rice itself would be soothing enough. Cheap too. On the island there would be plenty of fish, Mark assured us. Ansti could hardly complain about fresh fish.

The Indian influence was strong in Port Sudan at that time, so many of the civil servants having been posted there after service in India. This had its bad side in set attitudes to the "locals" and to non-British businessmen. Even the few British in business there were referred to as "commercials," a second-grade sort of people to "administrators." "Memsahib-ism," Mark told us, was also very noticeable, particularly in the British Club. I had read enough Kipling to appreciate what this meant and the disdain in his voice. Memsahibs (wives), then generally drawn from the untraveled and unimaginative British middle classes, were far more intolerant and snobbish than their men, and once supplied with servants to do everything in the house became domestic and social tyrants. In looks, Mark added, they also compared badly to the local girls, and they knew it. Husbands were kept on very short leads (leashes) and these wives were on the alert for slights everywhere. Mark was very against memsahibs. Other nationalities, he said, managed things much better and with more grace. I gathered in this case he was referring to the Greeks and Lebanese, there not being any other nationalities to consider in Port Sudan, apart from the Sudanese of course.

In a couple of days we were loaded into Mark's Bedford lorry, with Mark driving, us girls in the front beside him and Ansti, the cook Hassan and the driver Mohammed perched in the back. We ground very slowly over the rough track, mostly in low gear, heading for a Hadendowa settlement up the coast called Mohammed Qul, pronounced "ghoul." The island of Umsharifa lay four miles offshore. Mark kept his fishing boat in Mohammed Qul. The boat, he said, was an example of the ridiculous procurement policies of the Colonial Office. "A herring drifter! What the hell did they send me a North Sea herring drifter for out here?" Mark had been a punt-gunner then a commercial fisherman in Poole in Dorset and had very strong opinions about boats. I knew nothing about a herring drifter's specifications but gathered it was wrong in every possible respect for a boat operating in the tropics as a "mother boat" for pearl divers, which is what Mark was supposed to be doing: teaching the local fishermen to dive for pearl shell using aqualungs. Mark was convinced that aqualungs were "the answer" to the development of this fishery, but I wondered. A sandy uninhabited 120 miles lay between M.Q. and the P.W.D. workshops in Port Sudan, and what did the P.W.D. know about aqualung maintenance anyway? Weren't aqualungs a bit tricky to maintain? Divers would depend for their lives (and livelihood) on oxygen cylinders with complicated valves and, I was sure, other stuff that wouldn't work gummed up with sand and dirt. Even Ansti was still doing his diving in a helmet at the end of hose attached to an air compressor, and even this was subject to breakdown. But Mark insisted that he was imparting all the training he himself had received at Siebe-Gorman, that the Hadendowa fishermen were natural divers, that the prospects were great and so on, and his enthusiasm was hard to resist. The locals were gung-ho for the advantages the free-ranging aqualungs would give them, he said. What was so difficult about setting up a workshop and training someone to run it? Was I thinking like a memsahib and assuming no local could possibly be clever enough?

Of course I did not want to be caught thinking like a memsahib. God forbid!

"The Fuzzy-Wuzzies broke the British square at Omdurman, don't forget," Mark added with finality. (The Hadendowa and the Fuzzy-Wuzzies, named for their hair style, were the same people.) In this way we passed the time on the way to the island, while Ansti chewed his nails and the cook and driver slept soundly in the hot sun, their head-cloths over their faces.

In Mohammed Qul Mark's fishermen transferred everything from the lorry to his boat, which we now got a good look at. There was an enclosed wheelhouse and very little deck space. Below deck the "accommodation" consisted of a small cabin containing four stacked bunks with a solid fuel stove at one end of it, no doubt cozy in the North Sea. There was no hatch for air and only four feet of "headroom" and it was unbelievably hot. As far as Mark was concerned, this so-called cabin was a waste of good hold space, while the enclosed wheelhouse restricted visibility. He was nearly as scornful of the civil servants in the Colonial Office in charge of procurement as he was of memsahibs.

Still, it was transport. The engine worked and we anchored without incident off Umsharifa, a low, flat island with two tents on it, one for him and one for his men. Here there was at least a slight breeze and we could see beautiful coral heads either side of the sandy patch we had anchored in. We went ashore in a small local canoe and waded along the shoreline while Mark dug two more tents out of the baggage and Hassan behind his small shelter got the primus stove going to make some lunch. Mark may have got along well enough with Ansti but he had no intention of sharing his tent with him and had insisted on being issued with two more for this project. As he pointed out, the tents weren't being used then in any case: these were emergency shelters for pilgrims from the interior of Africa stopping near Port Sudan on their way to and from Mecca. and it wasn't "*haj* season." "The tents look it too, don't they?" Mark remarked. "Hassan keeps tearing loose bits off them to use as kitchen rags." Indeed we could see bits of tent flapping in the onshore breeze even at midday, and at night if the wind got up it proved quite noisy.

Hassan and his wind shelter

"Diving helmet practice, girls," Ansti decreed after we'd eaten. We discovered this consisted, for the time being, of us walking up and down the shore balancing the heavy helmet on our shoulders and at the same time trying to see what we were stepping on (fish bones, bits of sharp coral) through the Cyclops face plate. The metal shoulders, still unpadded, were very uncomfortable without water to take some of the weight, and the consequences of anything but a perfectly upright posture were painful. Too bad Mark's fishermen seemed to have nothing to do but watch this performance. Why didn't they go catch some nice fish?

Fortunately in the tropics days end early. We changed and were invited into Mark's tent for a drink before supper. In the tent he had placed the long low wooden table I'd last seen in Suakin with his stature of Kwan Yin again at one end of it. There were no chairs or stools (and no room for them either); we sat on local mats in front of the table near the entrance while Mark sat on the other side where, he explained, he kept his paperwork, his clothes, and his box of "hooch." His camp bed was set up behind him, swathed in a mosquito net. It was only a matter of time before Ansti would christen this set up a night club too.

Island Life

When we were not practicing with the helmet out of and in the water, we spent our time goggling, using Mark's snorkels and flippers, spending hour after hour drifting idly over the corals and watching the fish. The fish were very "tame" and unafraid. We were I think too big for them to identify and did not swim in the purposeful manner of a shark or a barracuda. Whole schools of small silver fish would flow over our bodies as over an inanimate obstacle; others, poking their heads out from among the sea anemones seemed to watch us calmly as they waited for something edible to float by. Under the larger coral heads lurked wide-mouthed rock cod (groupers), very territorial, Mark said, but shy. At any movement towards them, they withdrew quickly into their lairs. Mark had warned us what to beware of: sea urchins with long spines and the so-called "chicken fish" whose striped feathery fins carried an irritant poison, and in general we were careful not to touch anything. Just looking in that clear tranquil water was pleasure enough, and the contrast of the perfect slightly less than body temperature of the water with the hot desert air of the island ensured we spent nearly all day in the water, unless required for something else.

In a few days, letters from Ronald and Andrew and a great many anxious ones from home began to follow us up from Port Sudan, accompanied by a basket of fruit from Sidney. Sidney, fat and rather unprepossessing in person, was the kindest of the Port Sudan bachelors (temporary and actual) and managed to send up whatever fruit or vegetable he could find via passing lorries. Sam's "undying love," which had now, he claimed, been transferred from Gwen and Patricia to us, was far more self-centered. His notes said he was suffering but came without fruit. We knew his suffering was strictly temporary.

The arrival of letters meant more trouble with Pru over the diary business. I had thought it would all blow over, but Andrew had recently been down to Nairobi and mentioned it to Ronald, probably in rather strong terms, and even my mother had, by letter, become involved somehow. The consequent fuss brought old quarrels to the surface again and refreshed Pru's determination to "have everything out" with me. Ronald now maintained that he had only shown or read Pru my diary because it proved I was not a good friend to her and deceitful besides and he "thought she ought to know this."

Why? What good would come of it? With the diary business brushed under the carpet if not almost forgotten, we had been getting along rather well of late, and Pru had gradually become more her old self. Mark had said to me that once we got to the island and had lots to do, Pru would "cheer up," and he had been right.

On the Mau Mau front, Andrew's letter said he was now "out for" another Mau Mau "general," General Kago. He gave me a new address, in care of 4 Platoon G.S.U. in Manunga. He didn't say where Manunga was or if the area was worse than where he had been before. By worse, I meant more dangerous. As often before, I thought: what if he were killed? In the silent hours of the night, I examined my inner thoughts about this as honestly as I could and I knew that I would get over it. But should I have known this? Pru was once more telling me daily how shallow and deceitful I was, and with her eyes I looked at myself and didn't much like what I saw. I also compared my thoughts to Andrew's constancy and certainty and scored badly there too. On top of this, my mother's letters lectured me for "disrupting family loyalty" by criticizing Ronald to Andrew. Well! I wasn't the one who went about reading other people's diaries, I thought hotly. Anyway, what loyalty? According to both of them, separately, they disliked each other and always had. I was disgusted with the whole business. The idea of having Ronald as a brother-in-law was less appealing than ever. He might, or might not, marry Pru — Andrew thought he didn't seem much in love to him — but he was still going to be my brother-in-law. Nor had Ronald been pleased by this idea. His reaction to Andrew's and my engagement had been to tell me curtly, "I'm sorry I can't congratulate you."

I was now careful not to leave any letters much less my diary lying around, and this necessity was disagreeable.

The island life was lovely, though, and I think we both fell under its spell. Simple watery days were succeeded by brilliant nights full of stars. Mark, Pru and I went for nightly walks around the periphery of the island, playing leap frog or standing on our heads, then listening to Mark's records while enjoying a nightcap, and sleeping soundly to the rhythmical flapping of bits of tent. But for Ansti, life on the island was much less happy. Even here he was plagued by his equipment. Mark provided a large shark (dead) easily enough, but something went wrong every time it was guided with sticks towards a "helpless" girl in her diving helmet. By the end of a week we had done very little filming with dead sharks and certainly were not ready to graduate to a live manta ray. Mark, who had been with the Italian film crew shooting *Il Sixto Continente* (the English version was called "The Blue Continent) as an adviser soon got fed up. He said the contrast between Ansti's working methods, let alone his equipment, and the Italians' was so great he did not believe Carapace would ever make a decent underwater film. To be fair, the Italians were a team of professionals. If a shot needed fifteen takes to get it as the director wanted it, that's what they did. Mark said they worked hard, all day, every day. Ansti was trying to be director and crew, his only assistants were amateurs (us) and his equipment cranky. He spent hours on the beach, brooding, we supposed, about what to do next, while we "stood by" in our white bathing suits. Mark would try to get a plan out of him first thing in the morning so he could then get on with his ordinary work. For three or four days he asked politely what he and his men could do. But he was not prepared to hang around for long and soon he stopped asking. Unless Ansti stopped him with some definite request, he upped anchor and left with his men for some pearl-filled bay further north. Ansti then complained to us that he was getting no help from the fisheries officer, and that without the use of the boat there was little he could do.

At the end of a week, Ansti got a lift in some merchant's lorry back to Port Sudan. He knew he had to get better equipment, though how and from where was not clear. Maybe he also went to complain about the unhelpful fisheries officer. "Let him," said Mark. He left Pru and me on the island, cheaper for him than any hotel and we did not complain. The waters around the island were playground enough for us. It was only sad that these beautiful coral gardens were of so little interest to Ansti compared to the corny confrontations between young females and large marine creatures of his imagination. It was the same old story of trying to net hippos and lions, but in far more pleasant surroundings.

Mark, who was very observant, at once took in the adverse possibilities of the one male and two females situation once we were left idle with no work to do. Via the same lorry in which Ansti had left, he invited one of the Ians to come while Ansti was away. He told me later (much later) that he had given this Ian strict instructions about which girl to pay attention to, but neither Pru nor I knew this and we had a jolly and equal time

While Ansti was in Port Sudan, he wrote my mother about how he was "$4000-5000" over budget just because we had left him and he had had to import Gwen. Then he had had to let Gwen go, he told her, because Gwen was "too absorbed in the men of the forest and not in the beasts, or," he added, "in the sea around us."

"I fear my 6000 feet of film is worthless. Disaffection of personnel put me in a disturbed state of mind. I could not get up the concentration necessary for exacting shots. I also lacked exsperience [sic] in this field." [referring here to his terrestrial efforts, I think].

"Is there any chance of having a room from you when I get back which I hope will be May to July?"

A few days later we got a note ourselves:

"I have everything except aqualung, extra outboard & harpoon gun. I have mail, package for P. Beaucoup groceries."

We wondered what "everything" meant if the outboard and harpoon gun were excluded, or maybe he had them but just not the aqualung? He would have had to send to Egypt to get an aqualung, if not further. Nevertheless we had some idea of another fresh start, another try. He had the help of Mark and his men for the asking, and two girls, all on one small island with no other distractions. All he had to do was make the camera work in its underwater casing, and in this surely he was a professional. Anyone who could invent the bathysphere was no slouch at underwater casings. My mother had always told me Ansti was a mechanical genius. I had seen little evidence of this so far, but somehow you go on believing what your mother tells you, don't you?

Another week went by. For four of the days the beautiful flat blue sea became rough; gray and opaque: a wind had got up and the action of the waves stirred the bottom sand. Hassan's cooking shelter blew down twice, also the matting around the latrine, and Mark worried the tents themselves might go. There was no shelter anywhere from the blowing sand, and of course Mark could not get any work done either. We all just had to sit it out. More mail came up the coast, a lot of it for Ansti. We wondered if it might contain a withdrawal of his permit to work here. The Sudan government, in the person of the administrator in Port Sudan, had issued definite orders that Carapace was not allowed to film or do anything else except under supervision, and Mark had been told he personally was responsible to the government for the safety of all personnel. But after one day of wind, Ansti was all set to move somewhere else, claiming he was wasting good filming time. Mark told him that apart from the odd blow there was nowhere better to be for a filming base than an island, and that anyway he wasn't allowed to move anywhere else by himself. There was a row. Mark also told him the Italians had taken half of their feature film a week. This did not improve Ansti's temper.

By this time we had plenty of evidence ourselves about how unsuitable for filming the diving helmet was: cumbersome and bulky on a girl and permitting no swimming shots. We reckoned that even Gwen would not have looked good in the helmet. Inevitably this led Ansti to ask ("demand" was more his tone) to use the government aqualungs. Mark was supposed to help him, wasn't he? He had aqualungs, didn't he? This request Mark refused out of hand. "I am responsible for the safety of everyone on this expedition. None of you have any training in the use of aqualungs, and in any case I cannot authorize your use of government equipment for your private purposes. If you were to get your own aqualung, I would try to see that Wendy and Pru were safe using it, but that's all I would do."

Ansti went off to his tent and Pru and I went to Mark's tent for a drink. We had been careful to buy several bottles of liquor in Port Sudan to contribute—it was too difficult to get beer carried up the coast—but generally we drank mostly tea. We sat around, playing records. We did this every evening and if Ansti could hear music over the noise the wind made, it must have enraged him even more. Mark told us it was definitely on the cards that the Carapace expedition would be refused further permission to stay. The help the government had already offered was a lot, and if Carapace chose to be difficult, he'd be "out." Like Gwen.

At the end of the blow, however, Mark allowed us all to go with him to Shab Shagara, where he was teaching the men to use aqualungs in a sheltered bay, good for finding pearl shell. He said that if this place suited Ansti better, he would consider moving camp. We found it not nearly as picturesque as Umsharifa, above or under the water, and being further up the coast the communications with Port Sudan were even less frequent than from Mohammad Qul. We said nothing, but I guess Ansti agreed because he did not ask to go again. That night Mark caught another huge shark on his "shark line," a contraption made of shark hooks baited with whole fish attached by chains to a series of empty oil drums and finally to a large anchor. It was cruel, but efficient; once hooked, even a thrashing 2000 pound shark could not escape. Once again, Mark spent a few hours hauling the dead shark around by its tail while we pretended to be "attacked" and Ansti filmed. Of course the girl in the helmet could hear no instructions either from Mark or Ansti, although she could see, if facing the right way, a lot of mysterious hand gestures, and the least movement away from the perpendicular produced a surge of water and bubbles inside the face plate in place of air.

Towards the end of February Ansti left again for Port Sudan, giving no particular reason, and then instead of returning to Umsharifa, sent a message for us to return to Port Sudan too. We rode down in Mark's lorry wondering what was up now. We took all our things. You never knew with Ansti what you might be doing next, and where. It turned out that he planned to go to Massawa again to try to again to hire a launch or a "dow," as he spelled it, with a tender, so our expedition could be independent. He said he could not afford to have his filming held up by bad weather. How would our being on a dhow overcome poor underwater visibility? We decided it had become unbearable for him to be stuck on an island being supervised—told what he could and could not do. It was East Africa all over again.

Needless to say the view of the British District Commissioner in Port Sudan was different, and once again the terms under which Ansti had been granted permission to film in the Red Sea off the coast of what was then the Anglo-Egyptian Sudan were carefully spelled out to him.

The District Commissioner did not at all like the sound of some dhow from Massawa, crewed by Eritreans who might not know the coast, and these Eritreans would all need entry permits. He would have none of it. We were naturally not present at this interesting interview, but the D.C. came along to the hotel afterwards and told us about it. The Fisheries Officer had been correct in all he had told Mr. Carapace, he said, and he warned us privately that if Carapace made any more of a nuisance of himself, administratively speaking, he would quickly follow Miss Randall out of the country, and so would we.

He then revealed that only kindness, perhaps, he admitted, unwise kindness on his part, had prevented him from sharing the details of her unfortunate behavior in Port Sudan with the Governor's office in Kenya. If he had, she would not have got back into Kenya to marry her young man. We gathered there was some sort file passed between the administrations of places under colonial office rule identifying "undesirables." Lucky Gwen! She never knew how close she'd been to "non grata" status down the eastern coast of Africa. It was also rather scary. We wondered, not for the first time, if Ansti were taking the British Government seriously enough. He claimed, however, that the District Commissioner had had no objection to the dhow idea when he had first arrived in the Sudan, and that furthermore his personnel (that is, us) had been informed of this idea before we left Nairobi. The second part was true. Ansti had certainly mentioned launches and dhows to us, but Ansti had a lot of ideas that never came to anything so we had by that time become relaxed about the implications of any one idea in particular. At least, I had. Pru was by nature more cautious, but even Pru took most things in her stride. Maybe neither of us at twenty-one (twenty-two now) had enough experience to appreciate the risks. And perhaps if those assigned to watch over us had been less personable we too might have felt, like Ansti, that this supervision was damned British nonsense getting in the way of independent American enterprise.

We were still hanging around Port Sudan a week later. In the first few days of March, there was a flurry of communications to us from Ansti on his favorite lined green paper. On March 3rd (a Wednesday) he wrote,

"Dear Wendy, I have been meaning to write to say how sorry I am to have quarreled with a man who means so much to you. I should be happy if these things could be forgotten…It looks as though we might go to Mohammad Qul by lory[sic] again Friday. Have you check[ed] perishable groceries. Two more cases have arrived. I plan to return [to Port Sudan] about March 15th by which time all our equipment will be here. To be sure this is four months late. I could say that your running away and the getting of Gwen caused everything, but there is no doubt I contributed a lot of negligence to the picture.

Later the same day, another green note said,

"Please avoid arrangements that tend to split up our expedition. A united front is desirable for esprit de corpse [sic]."

On March 4th we received a rather acid note:

"By direction of D.C. we will not start until Saturday morning [it was then Thursday]. Do not hesitate to ask me to postpone a departure for private reasons of your own, but please remember how far behind schedule we are." In this note, he also re-introduced the Expedition Table" idea.

At the same time, he wrote Mark a formal letter addressed to "Mr. Veevers-Carter."

"With trade winds blowing and necessity for sheltering under a lee, I believe I must get a fairly large boat and awning under my control.

"If a launch cannot be found, I must resort to a dow or fold up. I estimate two to four months' work once we get started which I hope will not be later than March 15th.

Assuring you of my desire to cooperate and thanking you for your assistance, Anstruther Carapace."

It was more than time for me to get a letter off to my mother to try to explain what was going on, with Ansti and with me personally. I had reached a big decision.

"March 6th 1954 Port Sudan
"Dear Mother
"Sorry not to have written these past days since we have been in Port Sudan, but so much has been changing, personally as well as where the expedition is concerned, that it's hard to keep up. Ansti has been offending government officials right and left, and he's finding out that in the Sudan this is not treated casually…

You know, we all thought that on the familiar territory of doing undersea work Ansti would improve, but he's worse. Mark, the government, Pru and I now all think it would be better should the whole thing fold up – that he should be denied permission to continue for what he plans really does sound dangerous.

"We have tried to be wiser this time, however. There have been no scenes. But maybe our passive resistance technique has been equally effective in driving this poor unhappy man out of his mind? It's hard to tell. He does not listen to what is said to him either publicly or privately.

"Right now Mark is drafting a letter to the D.C. to say that he no longer wants to have the responsibility of this expedition, and that for the safety of all personnel, it would be better if such permits he has already been granted were revoked. I think Mark is writing you as well and sending you a copy of his official letter

"Later: it looks as if we will all be going off somewhere tomorrow after all, in spite of everything, but for how long I don't know. Mark's boss, the Game Warden Col. F. is due here Sunday. Then things will begin to pop. If I could give you a date when things will actually fold up, I would. A week? Two weeks? Two days? But you must have given up long ago trying to get definite plans and dates out of anyone on the Carapace safari.

"I suspect that if Ansti is closed down, he will blame it all on us. He was telling one of the amiable bachelors here only last night how he had 'been mistaken in those girls.' He had thought we were 'career girls' – i.e. not interested in men? – but he'd had "nothing but trouble with us since we came to Africa.'

There's something else I've been putting off telling you, mother—something that may relieve you or may shock you, but which has taught me a lesson. I know now that I am not really in love with Andrew. I gave him all my love at the time, and really believed it myself, but God, mother, what an ass I've been. You are so right about traveling and the stresses and strains to which one is subjected...

"I am still convinced that my life with Andrew could be happy. We are well-suited and certainly we were in love. But I know now that it was not all it could have been. It came as a shock, and it hurts me to think of how much I will be hurting him, but I can't go through with it. I feel a fool. Your plans are so far advanced. I'm letting everyone down.

"I feel so different now. I feel I have learned a lot in the time we've been on the island, with time to think and realize that my heart was filled more with an idea than with Andrew himself. He is too good, in a way. I can't honestly say I did not have doubts before, but I thought that one had to look at what life offered and select what one valued most and that out of this one can make a happy marriage. One can—but one can't make *the* marriage.

"How hard it is to be honest with oneself—to realize that even if one takes a long time to decide, hovering on the brink of deciding for months, the way I did, that the decision might in the end not be the right one.

"Everyone at home will think I'm a fool.

"Pru has been very sweet and kind about all this. She says she now knows how I felt when I was with her and Oliver in Mombasa. There has been no more trouble between us lately. She says she is going to wait and go home first before deciding whether or not to marry Ronald...."

I was sure that my mother would reasonably expect me to do the same. But my fourteen page letter was disingenuous, deliberately disingenuous. I was putting off the storm I knew would break over my head if I told my mother baldly, at this point, that I had decided to marry not Andrew but Mark. It had taken her months to come around to the idea of Andrew, but she had adapted. He had written her good letters, she said. She would be unhappy to have her only child so far away, but she accepted my choice. Now I was throwing all this over without warning. I lacked the courage to add that my choice was now some other game ranger person about whom she knew nothing except that he crept about a dead city at night in an opera cape, plus the bits I had casually passed on about his adventurous life up to now, and none of tales were of a nature to make an anxious mother comfortable. A commercial fisherman in Poole harbor? A farming assistant? Crew on a sailing boat to the West Indies? Then Captain (on a local ticket) of a sailing ship working cargo down the east coast of South America, through the straits of Magellan, dismasted there in a storm, jury-rigged to Tahiti where he'd quarreled with the ship's owners over how to get back (they would not pay the cost of taking the boat through the Panama Canal, he said, and he wasn't going through those bloody straits again), then while waiting for a new mast to be shipped out, beachcombing in the Marquesas. None of this, even edited, sounded any respectable or reliable notes. Nor did he have a war record like Andrew's: he'd been too young to join up until the end, when he got into Air-Sea Rescue in some lowly position, not as an officer. No university degree either. My mother was very keen on academic qualifications, an idea Mark discounted in favor of practical experience. I don't think I even mentioned his time as a rubber planter in Malaya during the Communist "emergency." That after all this "knocking about" he'd had the nous to get himself a job as a fisheries officer in the Colonial Service did not weigh much in the balance. I knew what she would say when told that I planned to share his island life of boats and tents in the Red Sea, a life lived entirely in bathing suits as far as my mother could make out, with no plan for "the future." In 1954 the Sudan was just starting to rumble uneasily with "independence." British government servants were being "Sudanized" and there was already unrest in the large Christian southern Sudan over its inevitable rule by Moslem northerners when the Anglo-Egyptian administration pulled out. The future? What future?

All my mother had heard about Andrew made him sound "steady" and all she heard and would hear about Mark—from me, who was probably putting the best gloss on it—made Mark sound the opposite.

On top of this was the probable breakup, a final breakup, with Anstruther. She would have to pick up the pieces there too. The next letter I got announced she was flying out. She would try to come in April, she said, stopping off in Cairo to visit earnest, intellectual archaeological friends, on the way. She obtained from me a promise to travel with her for a while in Europe or somewhere and to go home with her afterward, and meanwhile to do nothing rash (more rash) right now. She would "see to" Pru as well, she said. Pru's parents were not going to fly out to the Sudan, but then they did not think they'd had to in order to "get her back." Pru was now looking "steady" too, unlike me.

I pretended to be happy about her plans, but I had serious misgivings. Mark was in every respect not Andrew and could be very provocative when attacked and I knew my mother would attack him on arrival if not five minutes after. Seeing how the land lay he would then pretend to be even more outrageous than usual, just for fun. There was going to be a lot of unpleasantness and I dreaded it. If I had known just how unpleasant it was going to be and for how long, I might have lacked the courage to stand up to her. You might as well try to stand up to a maddened buffalo charging in defense of its calf.

I also (deservedly I know) received another blow. Before I had nerved myself to write Andrew, Andrew wrote me an angry, furious diatribe full of hurt and incredulity. Pru had been sweet to me, to my face, about my change of mind but she had also written Ronald about it in great detail and Ronald had at once passed her letter on to Andrew. He would, wouldn't he? And "telling all" was so like Pru. I had really been stupid. I don't know why it had not occurred to me that she might do this. Pru had even written her parents about Mark, and they had called my mother, so my careful "reasonable" letter was too late.

March 6th was also a busy literary day for Ansti. He wrote a letter to my mother's lawyer. Not everyone's mother "has a lawyer" but my mother did, for business reasons, and as she always made friends of her advisers, legal, financial, or medical, these people became closely involved in her personal life. My personal life too. She was a widow; though by no means a helpless widow, and though not overly fond of taking advice, she still liked to have plenty of it available. My father had died when I was four, but I sometimes felt I had about twenty substitutes whom my mother could always produce to tell me what to do, or, usually, that what I was doing was wrong.

Ansti now made use of the lawyer. He told Basil (the current lawyer) about our behavior and reviewed our past sins, and repeated his claim that yes, he had agreed to pay the two of us $5 per day but only for a working day, not a "day spent sitting around a hotel." We had already conceded that this might be reasonable if time spent "sitting around the hotel" was our fault. If the constant delays and changes of plan were Ansti's fault, we thought he ought to pay the bills. This had been a long-standing argument and had never been satisfactorily resolved. Sometimes he won, sometimes we won. He was now seeking (at no cost to himself) a legal opinion, one which would weigh heavily with my mother. He now proposed not to pay us anything for the time we had been left on the island. There was also, still outstanding, the question of our trajectory through Ethiopia. Air tickets, yes; hotels, even the dumps at Dessie and Adigrat, no. Asmara, no. Pru was especially exercised by this. What had started out as a jolly jaunt to Africa for a meager salary but, as she and I had both thought, "all in," was proving expensive. I had been given a slightly better allowance than she had, and was less surprised by Ansti's behavior, but money was always causing some kind of strain between us over where to stay or eat, what to see or do. She was in a constant fury at Ansti's meanness, as she saw it, while I could see he was struggling against a great many odds, one of them financial. Besides, I would say, we're in Africa, aren't we? This had been O.K. in the Oliver days but was wearing thin now.

Ansti's letter to Basil was very long. He brought up the Expedition Table business, too, his main complaint being, as it had been in the beginning all those months ago, that he was generally left to eat by himself. We thought that if Basil could see his table manners he would be instantly sympathetic. But from a distance of some 12,000 miles Basil was asked to give a ruling on this idea in principle. Ansti said that if we ate at other tables he proposed debiting our account for the cost of "keeping us" for the whole of that day. Was he, he wanted to know, legally justified? To give Ansti credit where it is due, he sent me a copy of this letter.

He also went on to rehearse how we had "run away" and so on, and how he had had to bring out the much more expensive Gwen, from Hollywood, no less. He now told Basil that all that extra expense had been for nothing: Gwen had proved to be "an invalid" (!) and "unable to do the job." He did not add anything about her interest in men in spite of being a career girl.

In his last paragraph he remarked that the "crazy shipping situation" in the Red Sea was also costing him time and money delaying the arrival in Port Sudan of equipment he'd left in various places like Nairobi and Massawa. Still, he said, given two more months he was sure he'd get good film footage somehow. There was no mention of dhows or of his differences with local government officials.

I wrote quickly my mother ("reasonable letter number two") about Mark. I wanted to tell my side of the story. But while we were waiting in Port Sudan, I was pretty well at Pru's mercy. We had many long talks which got nowhere but from which I supposed she derived satisfaction. I did not berate her for telling Ronald and her parents about my faithless behavior. How could I? I had been faithless. Mark had charmed me as though I had never been "engaged." I had told him right away I was engaged but he had paid no attention and during the week one of the Ians was with us I hadn't shown any proper reluctance either. It was probably true that I was shallow. Maybe worse. A good time Charlie. A flirt. Anything for a fling? Not only that. I had betrayed Andrew just when his life was in danger and he needed to concentrate on staying alive (and catching Mau Mau generals). Wartime tales of those floosies who went out with other soldiers the minute their own men had gone off to the front went through my head. I had only been fourteen when World War II ended, but I remembered the stories.

I decided to test myself: to see if I was a real whore of whom no one could expect a decent constancy.

There was a "commercial" type who came to the hotel sometimes, a good-looking man, married with a wife actually in Port Sudan. He was an excellent tennis player, and as his wife did not play, he was always looking for partners. I gathered from others that "looking for partners" was not necessarily confined to the tennis court and I had of course noticed his flirtatious manner. One evening, I gave him an opportunity somehow to "make a date," and it wasn't for tennis. He said he would meet me in a certain place behind the Secretariat building, always deserted late at night. After Pru and I had gone upstairs, I made some excuse to go down again and slipped out of the hotel through a side door. I was beginning to hate myself properly by then, and I was also afraid. I had never done such a thing before, and he was a big, strong man (all that tennis). Staying in the shadows I flitted around the back of the secretariat building until I saw his car. Opening the door, I got in. He grinned and put his arm around me. "I thought you'd come," he said. He pulled me towards him hard and kissed me.

I immediately discovered something: I was not that much of whore. I wanted only to escape. I pushed him away. "Come on," he said, "what's the harm?"

"I can't stay. I have to go. I just have to" I babbled rather incoherently. I opened the door quickly and ran. I was so relieved he hadn't tried to stop me that I ran all the way back to the hotel and fled up the stairs only pausing outside our room door to quiet my breathing. I opened the door to find Pru asleep. Thank God. I undressed silently and got into my bed.

I wasn't sure just how much better this incident made me feel. Only a little, I think. I had still behaved badly. But I didn't, couldn't, change my mind about Mark. I was really in love this time. Mark, who had more experience, said he was too, and it was all settled between us. There only remained everyone else, Andrew. friends, family, and my mother. I wrote everyone letters which seem silly and naïve to me now about how sure I was this time and how wonderful Mark was and how much I regretted making a mistake before. I am sure no one believed a word. At best, perhaps they pitied me a little. "Poor dear. She's so *young*."

Meanwhile, there was Ansti. He now said we would return to Umsharifa with the few bits of equipment due to arrive, but without a dhow. He understood he would not be allowed to import a dhow but believed this prohibition had somehow come from us on safety grounds. He kept harping on this idea. holding this grudge against us, and became more cantankerous than ever. On our side, we could not help but be relieved. We could picture well enough a scene on a distant reef with Ansti shouting alternately at us and at a bunch of uncomprehending Eritreans and the whole show at the mercy of his erratic equipment. Mark said he had his orders and it wouldn't happen but we weren't convinced. Still, we went back to the island willingly enough (at least I was very willing) to give the film a last chance. Pru's lodestar was her airfare home.

But now everything and everyone was pushing in the other direction, towards a final break up. Even the outboard was temperamental. I now know that this is quite normal for outboards and maybe Ansti knew it too, but it used to send him into paroxysms of rage and frustration.

Mark kept telling us we had to "stop this nonsense." Resign, he told us. "If you won't work for him, he'll have to fold."

We muttered about air fares and promises, but Mark said that if we believed Carapace's promises we were as crazy as he was. Did we have a formal contract? No? "Well, there you are! You're both crazy, and I have something better to do, like my job. For heaven's sake, bring this circus to an end. Just resign!"

On March 27th after a particularly disagreeable confrontation on the beach when I told Ansti to shut up and he said he wished he could lick me and we all threw water and sand at each other like a bunch of school children, we did resign. We shouted, "we're resigning!" We told him nothing was working, everything was a waste of time and a few other things, and he did a lot of shouting too about our ruining his film and so on and we all went off separately to brood on what next.

My Mother Arrives to Sort Us All Out

By the time my mother arrived in Port Sudan, refreshed by a pleasant time in Cairo and actively determined to see to Ansti and both of us girls, we were back in Port Sudan with no job, no salary and no passage home. Although we weren't on speaking terms with Ansti, we were still getting notes from him about our breach of promise and unreasonable behavior. He said he believed we were just bored (!) He said I just wanted to see my friends in England.

I don't know how Pru felt about England, but I was not at all keen to go to England to face the chorus of disapproval already building up there about my misdeeds "Poor dears" were going to be as scarce there as they would be in the States. My mother had rounded up all her advisers and friends and all our relatives to write to me, and the opprobrium was already flooding in. I had been trusted. But I had betrayed the trust of both a good man and my poor mother. My mother was being driven frantic by my irresponsible behavior and my ingratitude for all the things she had done for me, even allowing me to go to Africa in the first place. After spending her money, all that money, on my education, was I seriously proposing to run off with some bearded lunatic to live on a desert island? Had I lost my mind? The least I could do was come home at once and behave myself. Grow up. Do something useful. Stop being such a spoiled brat. Your poor mother! If you really love this man in a year or two (a year or two at home, it went without saying), then your mother might consider you are really serious. And *if* he really loves you, they added slyly, he won't mind waiting. If he says he won't wait, then he doesn't really love you and you'd better wake up right now.

Mark and I discussed all this. He said he had absolutely no intention of waiting. "What for? For you to drag around New York City being hounded by your mother while I sit out here or somewhere waiting patiently for her permission to marry you? I won't do it, and that's that. We're in love, we get married, we get on with our lives together. Anything else is just a stupid waste of time and much too hard on both of us to be considered. Your mother doesn't like me, you can see that and so can I. She is unlikely to change her mind. All she wants is the time to make you change yours."

I had to agree. Romantic tales of lengthy engagements and long partings had no appeal to me either. I had promised "a trip" with my mother and to go home, but not how long I would stay there. Provisionally we agreed to meet in England in July when Mark would be due some home leave.

Pru's parents sent out an air ticket for her, and my mother an I got on a boat and went to Palestine. Not for religious reasons; I think she thought it would be improving, and it was geographically handy.

Ansti, robbed of the chance to finish his underwater film, surprisingly did not hold a long-term serious grudge against me, or Mark. After we had married, he wrote to say he was glad I was happy, and that in this case he now had no regrets having taken me to Africa. Would I like his old outboard motor as a wedding present? It was still in Port Sudan. We didn't much want the outboard, but both of us thought this very big of him, and agreed to forget the many accusations and disagreements.

Loose Ends

Pru stayed in the States. She did not marry Ronald but chose instead a fellow American, a doctor. I completely lost touch with Gwen. She was not a letter-writer, and the life I subsequently led abroad was dependent on letters. I would have liked to know if things worked out for her. She deserved some luck.

Andrew married a girl he met in Nairobi that year and, having decided against a farm, stayed in government service, at first in Uganda. By 1970 he had moved to Ethiopia under U.N. auspices as Game Warden for the Emperor, Haile Selassie.

Mark and I were living on an island in the Seychelles by then with our three children. In January, 1970, Mark went to Mombasa for dental treatment and died there in the dentist's chair. "Anaesthetic accident," said the report. He was still young, only forty-two. For some time I was unable to believe he'd gone. When Andrew heard about it in Ethiopia through a mutual friend, he wrote me a polite letter of condolence.

Nine years later, after his divorce, Andrew and I got married after all. He forgave me for running off, which was big of him too, and my mother in her old age breathed a sigh of relief.

And Anstruther?

At first, in the winter of 1954, he was determined to try again to finish his film in the Sudan. He wrote Mark that he had permission to do this from the Minister of Animal Resources, and had therefore left his boat, cameras, generator, diving gear, camping equipment etc. in storage at Mohammed Qul. But by the end of August he wrote again to say the permission had been withdrawn and no reason given. If this decision could not be reversed (and he asked Mark to try to reverse it), he'd probably be coming out to the Sudan to pick up his scattered equipment and go elsewhere. In that case. would Mark arrange to sell his small boat for him?

In spite of discouragement and the expense of collecting his equipment, some in Mohammed Qul, some in Massawa, and some in Nairobi, he still did not entirely give up. In October he wrote to say that although his "undersea black and white opus" had been superseded by Hans Hass's and Captain Cousteau's color pictures, he had "written to the usual sources for another mermaid." For the services of a mermaid, he was still offering $5 a day plus 2% of his gross "if she sticks to the end." He said he now had a much better "outfit: two 25hp. Johnsons, two aqualungs etc. "I hate to think of the time I wasted for W & P with all the old junk."

He sent us a provisional shooting schedule:

| ""Feb – Mar | Tulara, Peru - Giant squid at night. Automatic pelagraptor. |
| ""June – July | Belize – sawfish v. shark." |

He did not explain what a "pelagraptor" was. Something to grab marine sapecies in the open sea? Perhaps it was a gadget in the process of being invented.

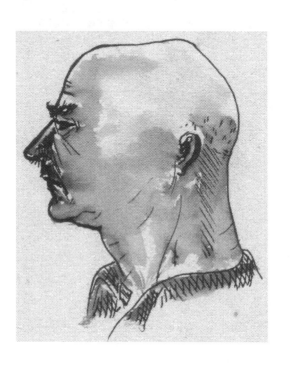